the LifePlan

A Guide to Multiply Disciple-Makers

plethosglobal.com

The Life Plan© content is property of Plethos Global™.

This content contained within this document may be copied and / or recopied. This document may not be edited, altered or sold without permission from Plethos Global™. Unless otherwise noted scripture quotes taken from The Holy Bible: New International Version © 1978, 1979, 1984 by International Bible Society & The Holy Bible, English Standard Version © 2001 by Crossway. Manual layout & design by Absolutely Unprofessional.

First Printing Life Plan© Virtual Disciple-Maker™ © 2018

Second Printing Life Plan© Plethos Global™ © 2019

ISBN 978-0-9997832-2-1

THE LIFE PLAN

Welcome to the disciple-making adventure of a lifetime! Plethos is part of a movement bringing discipleship and mission into the home. We believe that the Life Plan you are about to go through will equip you to be a disciple-maker with those in your home and circle of influence. At Plethos, we don't simply create content, but attempt to live the Life Plan daily as we cheer you on, pray for you and make ourselves available to coach you through this content as needed.

The first part of the Life Plan covers the Overview, our disciple-making commitment and rhythm of life. This section also covers our Current Reality, where we are today in our current walk with Christ at the start of the Life Plan.

The second section in the Life Plan is the Disciple-Maker Preferred Future for every family and local church. We believe that if every follower of Jesus embodied the six Preferred Future statements it would truly change our homes, our churches, and our communities. We know there could be many more statements to focus on, however, we believe these six are the essentials.

The third part of the Life Plan is the Disciple-Maker Pathway. These are the tools and habits to help achieve our goal, our vision, our preferred future. Again, there are many more tools we can add to our tool belt as we build a discipling culture in our home and circle of influence, yet, we focus simply on six essentials.

Every person, group, and family is unique. The content does not need to be taught in any particular order, but we do suggest integrating our Big Three Keystone Habits into your life rhythm:

1. Systematic Bible Reading and having a way to hold yourself accountable to practice what you learn.

2. Learning and applying Galatians 2:20 *(Living the Life of Christ)*.

3. Passing on what you are learning in your home and / or circle of influence.

We believe if you learn, live, and pass on this Life Plan to others it will help families win for generations. If you have questions you can always reach out to us at *plethosglobal.com*.

We are praying for you,
the Plethos Team

TABLE OF CONTENTS

The Life Plan: A Guide to Multiply Disciple-Makers

Overview & Current Reality

The Disciple-Maker's Commitment 3

The 4 Ds Diagram 5

The Life Plan 9 / Diagram 12

The Life Plan Evaluation 13

The Big Three Keystone Habits 19 / Diagram 22

Top 5s 25

The Greatest Danger 27

The Characteristics of Sin 31

True Grace 39 / Diagram 42

The Disciple-Maker Preferred Future

We Are Statement 1   48

We Are Statement 2   49

We Are Statement 3   50 / Diagram 51

We Are Statement 4   52

We Are Statement 5   53

We Are Statement 6   54

The Disciple-Maker Pathway

Living the Life of Christ 59 / Diagram 64

Matthew 6:33 Practice 67

Systematic Reading of the Bible 73
- Bible Reading Plan 74
- How to Study the Bible 75 / Diagram 81
- The Student, the Fish & Agassiz 83

The 8ight Priorities 89 / Diagram 92

Milk of the Word 95 / Diagram 126
- Introduction 96
- Repentance from Dead Works 98
- Faith in God 101
- Baptisms 104
- Laying on of Hands 108
- Resurrection of the Dead 110
- Eternal Judgement 115

Meat of the Word 119 / Diagram 126

PART I

Overview & Current Reality

THE DISCIPLE-MAKER'S COMMITMENT

Our Plethos Commitment to You

- ☐ **We are** going to start on time.

- ☐ **We are** going to end on time.

- ☐ **We will** strive to be at every meeting.

- ☐ **We will** follow the 5 P's: **P**roper **P**reparation **P**revents **P**oor **P**erformance.

- ☐ **We will** be "Worded up" and "Prayed up."

- ☐ **We are** committed to promptly put into practice what has been taught.

- ☐ **We aim** to be an example for you to follow.

- ☐ **We will** be available to help you catch up if you must miss a session.

- ☐ **We will** be vulnerable and create a safe place to be authentic.

THE 4 Ds OF TRAINING HUDDLES

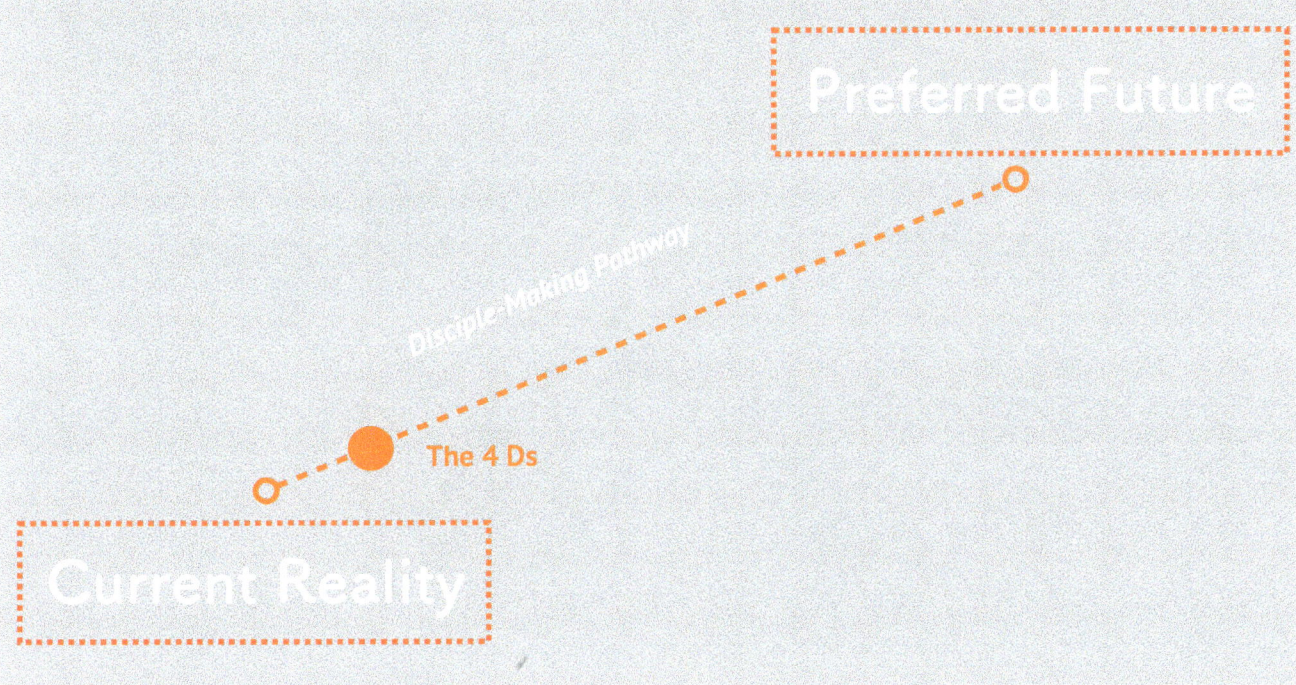

Why it Matters: Disciple-maker's are trained to offer clarity of the huddle format at the beginning of every training season.

The Life Plan is an integrated whole to be lived out by faith each day until it is the lifestyle of the disciple-maker.

THE 4 Ds of a Training Huddle

1. DEBRIEF — 15 min

This time is intentionally brief. It is for review and accountability.

- Review (Pete & Repeat)
- Accountability
- Life Updates
- Confession / Celebrating Wins

15 Minute **'Meeting Before the Meeting'** is a great way to connect with your group beyond the session.

2. DIG — 30 min

This time focuses on **Teaching and Discussion** where new material from the Life Plan is presented for the first time.

- Teaching the content (Life Plan Manual)
- Group participation / discussion / Q & A
- Illustrations (Coaches Guide)

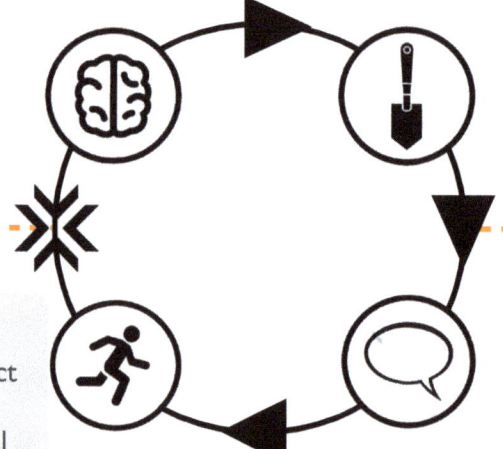

15 Minute **'Meeting After the Meeting'** is a great way to connect with your group beyond the session: answer Q's, offer personal insights, clarify content and pray together.

3. DISCUSS — 10 min

1. How am I to daily live?
2. How am I daily living?
3. What changes or growth do I need to make?

In 10 minutes connect the dots between the big idea of the DIG and the action of the DO.

4. DO — 5 min

DO one thing!

Encourage the huddle participants to pick one thing they are going to DO as a result of meeting together.

THE LIFE PLAN

Preferred Future

Disciple-Making Pathway

The Life Plan

Current Reality

Why it Matters: Clarity leads to confidence giving disciples the courage to put the Life Plan into action.

The Life Plan is an integrated whole to be lived out by faith each day until it is the lifestyle of the disciple-maker.

THE LIFE PLAN

From Your Current Reality to Your Preferred Future

Live it Out:

In our home. (Deut 6:4-7)

In our circle of influence. (2 Tim 2:2)

Intro to the Life Plan:

The Life Plan is God's way to help us live an eternally abundant and purposeful life in all circumstances. It is an integrated whole to be lived by faith each day until it becomes the disciple-maker's mindset. A lifestyle to be learned and lived out over a lifetime (John 10:10b; Romans 12:2b; John 3:16).

We've found that there are two primary relationship circles in which to train disciple-makers using the Life Plan:

1. In our home. (Deuteronomy 6:4-7)
2. In our circle of influence. (2 Timothy 2:2)

Our passion is to build the home using the Life Plan in order to help every faithful man and woman of God develop clarity, confidence, and the courage needed to train the next generation of disciple-makers. Imagine if every family in the church attempted to obey God expecting Him to fulfill their attempt with His power. We would have more and more healthy homes serving the local church. If our homes are built and rooted in Scripture we will inevitably build healthy churches equipped to help as many people as possible meet, know, and follow Jesus.

Remember, the Church is not a building, it is a movement of God we are called to be part of. We cannot go *to church* because the *church is you and me*. Since we are the church, the best way to live a Christ-like lifestyle is to begin training disciple-makers in the home and then within our circle of influence. We believe this will help families win at life to the fourth generation (Matthew 28:18-20; 2 Timothy 2:1-2).

The Disciple-Maker Preferred Future:

What you want to *BE* and *DO*. Disciples of Jesus on The Disciple-Maker Pathway, where each home is a training center.

- ☐ We are training disciple-makers. **Matthew 28:19-20**

- ☐ We are helping disciples train in godliness. **1 Timothy 4:7-8**

- ☐ We are helping each family unit be a love and truth center. **Colossians 2:6-8; John 13:34-35**

- ☐ We are distributing the grace of God by serving one another. **1 Peter 4:10**

- ☐ We are families on mission. **Matthew 28:19-20**

- ☐ We are teaching the consequences of not obeying Jesus. **Luke 6:46-49**

The Disciple-Maker Pathway:

Every adult and child is in the process of learning, living and being able to pass on to others, in their home and circle of influence, the Life Plan essentials.

- ☐ Know by heart *Living the Life of Christ*. **Galatians 2:20**

- ☐ Do *Matthew 6:33 Practice* everyday.

- ☐ Systematic reading of the Bible. **2 Timothy 2:15; 3:16-17; Acts 20:27**

- ☐ Living the *8ight Priorities*. **Matthew 6:33**

- ☐ *The Milk of the Word*. **Hebrew 5:11-6:2**

- ☐ *The Meat of the Word*. **Hebrews 5:13-14; Matthew 28:20; Romans 6:16**

THE LIFE PLAN DIAGRAM

Filling the G.A.P. / Growth. Achievement. Progress.

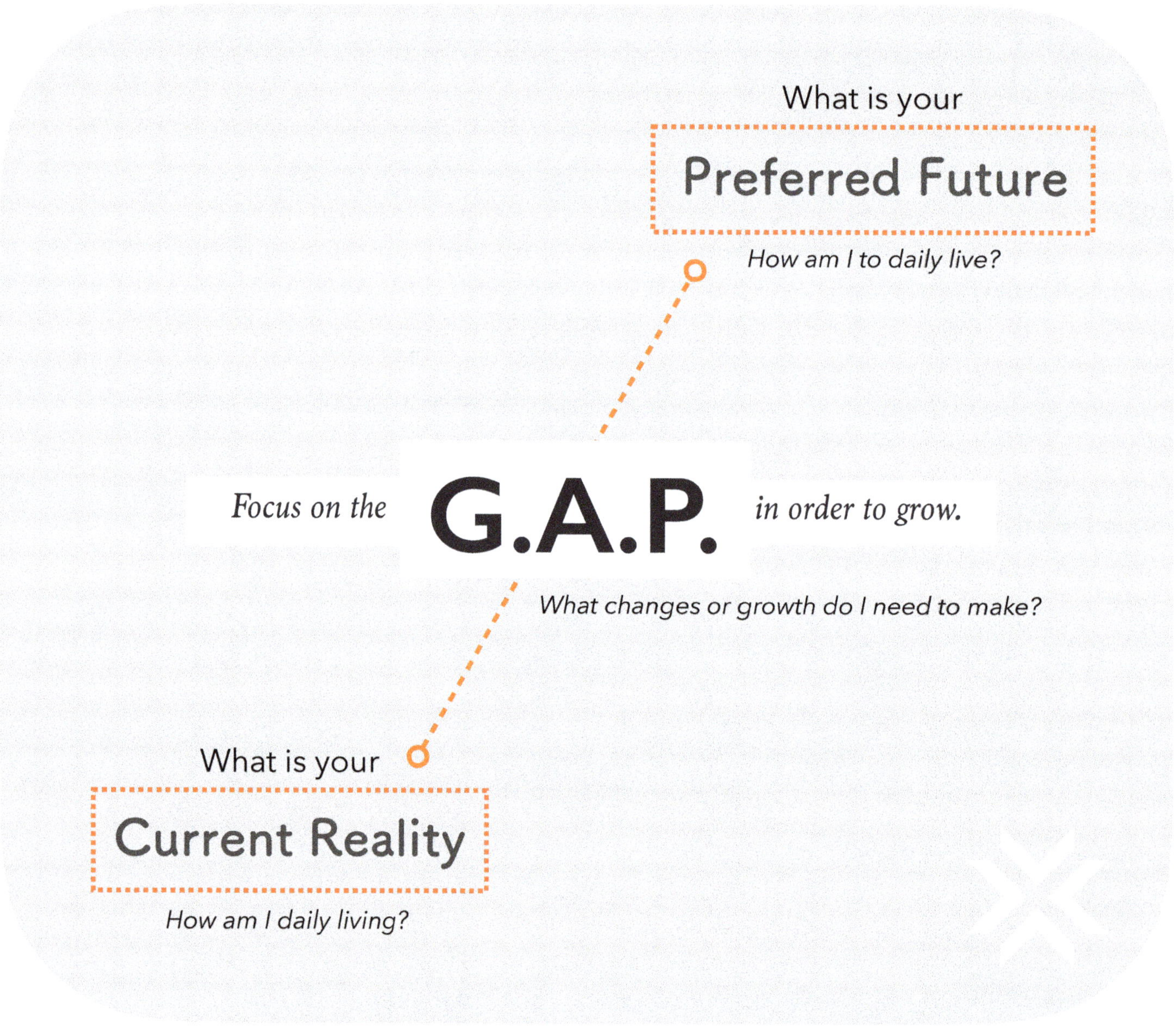

What is your

Preferred Future

How am I to daily live?

Focus on the **G.A.P.** *in order to grow.*

What changes or growth do I need to make?

What is your

Current Reality

How am I daily living?

THE LIFE PLAN EVALUATION

From Your Current Reality to Your Preferred Future

Acts 19:9-10

But when some became stubborn and continued in unbelief, speaking evil of the Way before the congregation, he withdrew from them and took the disciples with him, reasoning daily in the hall of Tyrannus from 11 AM to 4 PM ("from the 5th hour to the tenth"). This continued for two years, so that all the residents of Asia heard the word of the Lord, both Jews and Greeks.

INSTRUCTION

Take the following Evaluation.

Read each question and check the boxes that apply to you. There are three rows of boxes provided for each question designed to be taken multiple times throughout the training process. Be sure to date each row at the beginning of each evaluation for your records.

Hopefully this tool will help you discover what your next step is for each area as you evaluate what you have learned, are living out and are passing on to others.

(Date your evaluations to show progress)

PART 1 / The Disciple-Maker Preferred Future:

What you want to BE and DO. Disciples of Jesus on The Disciple-Maker Pathway, where each home is a training center.

▷ **We are training disciple-makers.** (Matthew 28:19-20)

- ☐☐☐ Are you intentionally investing your life in your children and/or in your spouse and/or your circle of influence? (Ephesians 6:4; 5:25; 2 Timothy 2:2)
- ☐☐☐ Are you teaching your children and/or spouse and/or your circle of influence how to invest their life in others?
- ☐☐☐ Are the people you are training intentionally investing in others?

▷ **We are helping disciples train in godliness.** (1 Timothy 4:7-8)

- ☐☐☐ Are you training daily in godliness? (learning and living God's Word)
- ☐☐☐ Are you training your children and/or your spouse and/or your circle of influence to train daily in godliness?
- ☐☐☐ Are the people you are training helping others train in godliness?

▷ **We are helping each family unit be a love and truth center.** (Colossians 2:6-8; John 13:34-35)

- ☐☐☐ Are you helping your local church become a love and truth center? (A place where you are learning and living the Word of God; displaying the qualities of love found in 1 Corinthians 13:4-8, 2 Timothy 3:16-17)
- ☐☐☐ Are you helping your home become a love and truth center?
- ☐☐☐ Are you training others to help their local church and their family be a love and truth center?
- ☐☐☐ Are the people you are training now training others to help their local church and family become a love and truth center?

▷ **We are distributing the grace of God by serving one another.** (1 Peter 4:10)

- ☐☐☐ Do you know what grace you have been given to give to others?
- ☐☐☐ Are you distributing the grace of God to the people who need it?
- ☐☐☐ Are you teaching those you disciple to distribute the grace they have been given by God?
- ☐☐☐ Are those you disciple teaching others to distribute the grace they have been given by God?

▷ **We are families on mission.** (Matthew 28:19-20)

☐☐☐ Are you a family on mission fulfilling Matthew 28:19-20?

☐☐☐ Are you teaching those you disciple to live as a family on mission?

☐☐☐ Are those you disciple teaching others to live as a family on mission?

▷ **We are teaching the consequences of not obeying Jesus.** (Luke 6:46-49)

☐☐☐ Are you helping your family understand the effects of disobeying Jesus' commands?

☐☐☐ Are you training your children to hear the words of Jesus and put them into practice?

☐☐☐ Are the people you disciple teaching the consequences of disobedience to God's Word?

PART 2 / The Disciple-Maker Pathway:

Every adult and child is in the process of learning, living and being able to pass on to others, in their circle of influence, the Life Plan essentials.

▷ **Know by heart *Living the Life of Christ*.** (Galatians 2:20)

☐☐☐ Are you learning and attempting to live the life of Christ found in Galatians 2:20?

☐☐☐ Are you teaching those you disciple Galatians 2:20?

☐☐☐ Are those you disciple teaching others Galatians 2:20?

▷ **Do *Matthew 6:33 Practice* everyday.**

☐☐☐ Are you learning and attempting to live out Matthew 6:33?

☐☐☐ Are you teaching those you disciple Matthew 6:33?

☐☐☐ Are those you disciple teaching others Matthew 6:33?

▷ **Systematic reading of the Bible.** (2 Timothy 2:15; 3:16-17; Acts 20:27)

☐☐☐ Are you systematically reading the Bible regularly?

☐☐☐ Do you have a way to hold yourself accountable for living what you learn?

☐☐☐ Are you teaching those you disciple to systematically read the Bible and have a way to hold themselves accountable to practice what they learn?

☐☐☐ Are those you disciple teaching others to systematically read the Bible and have a way to hold themselves accountable to practice what they learn?

▷ **Living the *8ight Priorities*.** (Matthew 6:33)

☐☐☐ Are you learning and attempting to live God's priorities?

☐☐☐ Do you know what areas you need help with?

☐☐☐ Are you accountable to anyone for living out God's priorities?

☐☐☐ Are you teaching those you disciple the Godly priorities?

☐☐☐ Are those you disciple teaching others the Godly priorities?

▷ ***The Milk of the Word.*** (Hebrew 5:11-6:2)

☐☐☐ Are you learning and attempting to live out the milk of the Word?

☐☐☐ Are you teaching those you disciple the milk of the Word?

☐☐☐ Are those you disciple teaching others the milk of the Word?

▷ ***The Meat of the Word.*** (Hebrews 5:13-14; Matthew 28:20; Romans 6:16)

☐☐☐ Are you learning and attempting to live out the meat of the Word?

☐☐☐ Are you teaching those you disciple the meat of the Word?

☐☐☐ Are those you disciple teaching others the meat of the Word?

THE BIG THREE KEYSTONE HABITS

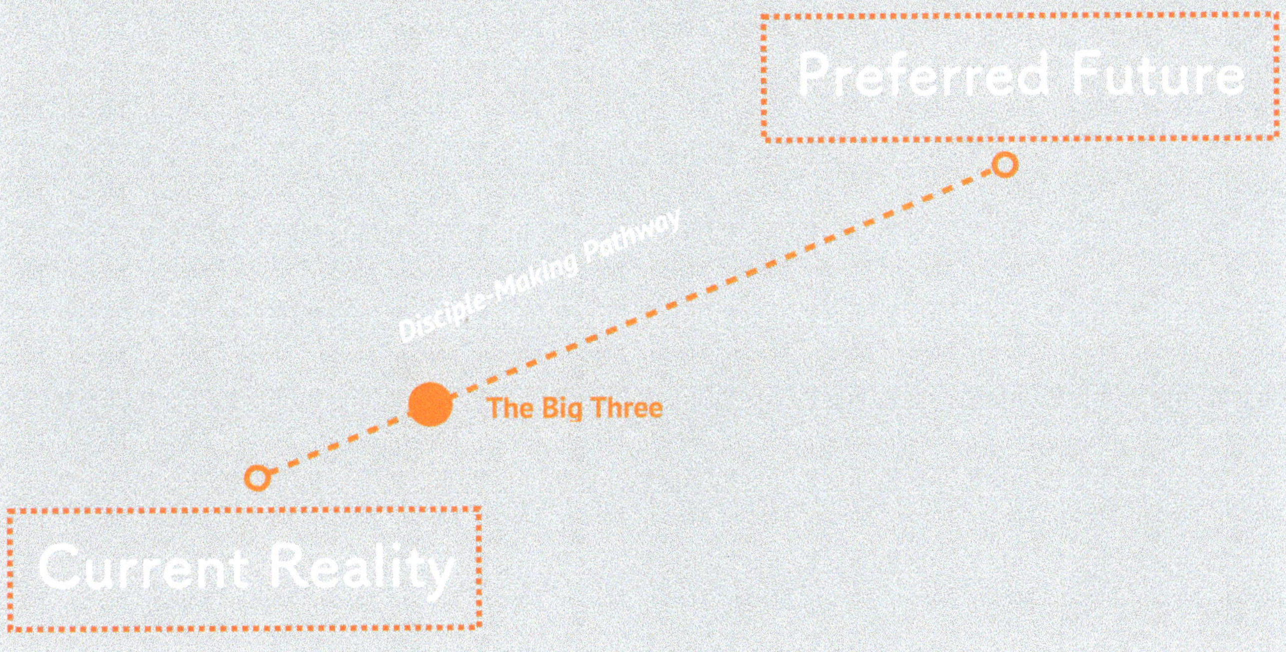

Preferred Future

Disciple-Making Pathway

The Big Three

Current Reality

Why it Matters: The Three Keystone Habits will transform our lives if we put them into practice daily.

The Life Plan is an integrated whole to be lived out by faith each day until it is the lifestyle of the disciple-maker.

THE BIG 3 KEYSTONE HABITS

Building Our Faith on Spiritual Habits

What is a Keystone Habit?

A keystone habit creates the domino effect for other areas of life. At Plethos, we believe The Big Three Keystone Habits are vital to a healthy lifestyle of following Jesus for the disciple and the disciple-maker.

Keystone Habit #1

THE WHAT: Systematic Bible Reading and having a way to hold yourself accountable to practice what you learn.

LEARN IT: What does God want me to BE and DO?

BIBLE: Christ calls us to become like Him and to follow in His footsteps on mission to the world around us. Spending time in His Word with a desire to know His love and truth and way of life more and more is a Keystone Habit for all disciples. (Joshua 1:7-8; 2 Timothy 3:16-17)

Practical Tool: Plethos *Bible Reading Plan*.

Keystone Habit #2

THE HOW: Learning and applying Galatians 2:20 (*Living the Life of Christ*).

LIVE IT: How do I become and act on what God wants me to BE and DO?

GOSPEL: This is what we call "Gospel Fluency." When we know the truth of Galatians 2:20 and are able to apply the truth of the **Galatians 2:20** document to every part of life each day, then we know we're living a Gospel-centered and Gospel-fluent lifestyle. (Galatians 2:20; 2 Timothy 1:13-14)

Practical Tool: *Living the Life of Christ* - Put to heart and mind the different elements of Galatians 2:20.

Keystone Habit #3

THE WHY: Passing on what you are learning in your home and / or circle of influence.

PASS IT ON: Why is it so important to pass on what we're learning to others?

MULTIPLY: Sharing what we're learning is a vital step in internalizing what we're learning as well as adorning the Gospel we're professing. Passing on Gospel truths is a key way for us to help families, including our own, win at life to the fourth generation. (Matthew 28:18-20; 2 Timothy 2:1-2)

Practical Tool: *The Top 5's List* is great way to begin praying for and engaging those in our family and circle of influence.

THE BIG ③ Keystone Habits

Building Our Faith on Spiritual Habits

Keystone Habit 1

THE WHAT: Systematic Bible Reading and having a way to hold yourself accountable to practice what you learn.

BIBLE: This one habit will change our lives. We have been given the words of life. Let's crave it and practice it with God's power (Joshua 1:7-8; 2 Timothy 3:16-17).

Practical Tool: *Plethos Bible Reading Plan*

LEARN IT: *What does God want me to BE and DO?*

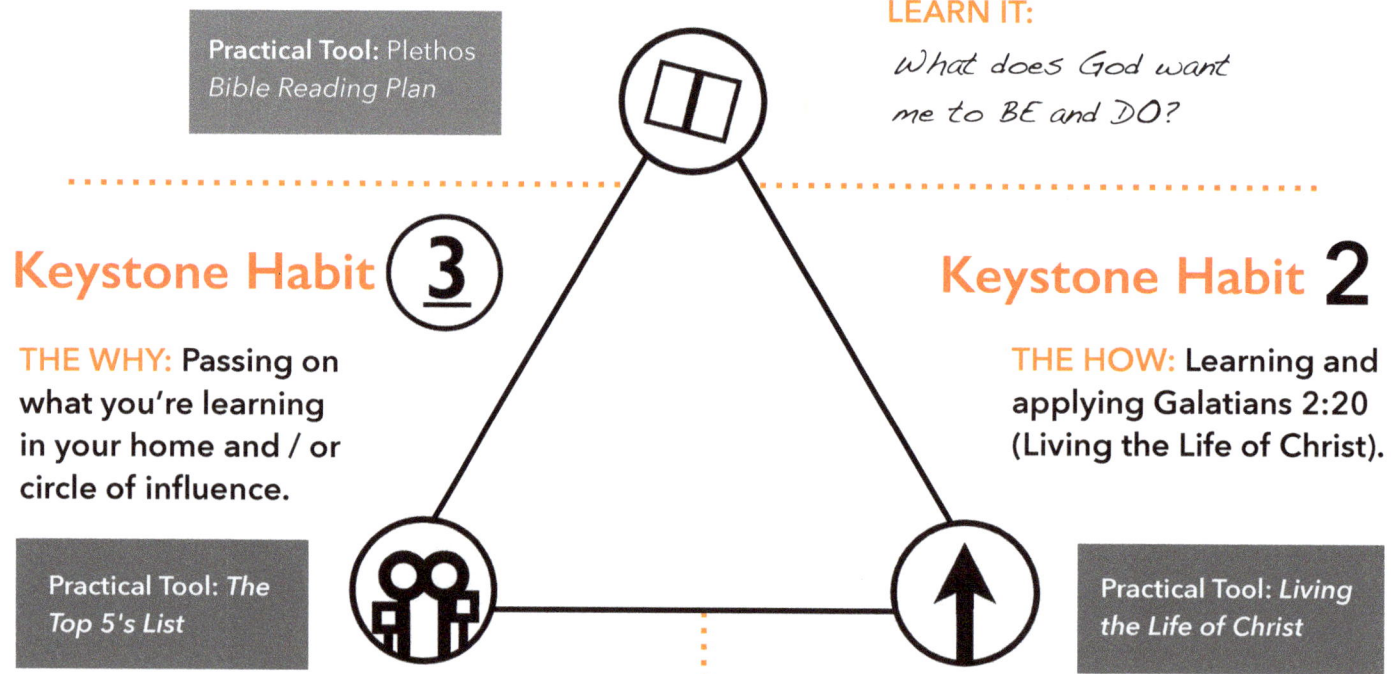

Keystone Habit 3

THE WHY: Passing on what you're learning in your home and / or circle of influence.

Practical Tool: *The Top 5's List*

Keystone Habit 2

THE HOW: Learning and applying Galatians 2:20 (Living the Life of Christ).

Practical Tool: *Living the Life of Christ*

MULTIPLY: Passing on Gospel truths is a key way for us to help families, including our own, win at life to the fourth generation (Matthew 28:19-20; 2 Timothy 2:1-2).

GOSPEL: This is what we call "Gospel-centered Living." When we know the truth of Galatians 2:20 and practice it, then we will begin to live a Gospel-centered lifestyle.

PASS IT ON: *Why is it so important to pass on what we're learning to others?*

LIVE IT: *How do I become and act on what God wants me to BE and DO?*

TOP 5s

The Five People You're Praying For

Who are your Top 5?

Create a short list of the Top 5 people in your home and circle of influence and pray for the opportunity to connect them to true life in Christ, walk through the Life Plan and impact their circle of influence.

1 _____

2 _____

3 _____

4 _____

5 _____

THE GREATEST DANGER

Preferred Future

Disciple-Making Pathway

Greatest Danger

Current Reality

 **Why it Matters:** Knowing sin is our greatest danger motivates us to seek safety in Jesus Christ.

 The Life Plan is an integrated whole to be lived out by faith each day until it is the lifestyle of the disciple-maker.

THE GREATEST DANGER

> **When did you learn how to cross the street?**
>
> What is the greatest danger we face in life?
>
> When did you learn it was the greatest danger?

Sin is the greatest danger we face because it leads to death

- **Romans 6:23** For the wages of sin is death, but the free gift of God is eternal life in Christ Jesus our Lord.

- **Hebrews 9:27** And just as it is appointed for man **to die once**, and after that comes judgment,

- **Revelation 20:11-15** Then I saw a great white throne and him who was seated on it. From his presence earth and sky fled away, and no place was found for them. ¹² And I saw the dead, great and small, standing before the throne, and books were opened. Then another book was opened, which is the book of life. And the dead were judged by what was written in the books, according to what they had done. ¹³ And the sea gave up the dead who were in it, Death and Hades gave up the dead who were in them, and they were judged, each one of them, according to what they had done. ¹⁴ Then Death and Hades were thrown into the lake of fire. This is the second death, the lake of fire. ¹⁵ And if anyone's name was not found written in the book of life, he was thrown into the lake of fire.

Sin causes us to experience physical and spiritual death with eternal torment, the second death.

Sin is the greatest danger we face because it leads to physical, emotional and relational breakdown

- **Galatians 5:19-21** Now the works of the flesh are evident: sexual immorality, impurity, sensuality, ²⁰ idolatry, sorcery, enmity, strife, jealousy, fits of anger, rivalries, dissensions, divisions, ²¹ envy, drunkenness, orgies, and things like these. I warn you, as I warned you before, that those who do such things will not inherit the kingdom of God.

- **Ephesians 4:31** Let all bitterness and wrath and anger and clamor and slander be put away from you, along with all malice.

- **James 4:1-2** What causes quarrels and what causes fights among you? Is it not this, that your passions are at war within you? ² You desire and do not have, so you murder. You covet and cannot obtain, so you fight and quarrel…

Physical, emotional and / or relational breakdown is caused by sin.

The Living & Written Word are our protection from sin's danger

- **Matthew 1:21** She will bear a son, and you shall call his name **Jesus**, for he **will save his people from their sins.**

    - Jesus, the Word (John 1:1, 14) saves us from the penalty (Romans 5:10), power (Romans 6:6-7) and presence (John 14:1-3) of sin.

- We receive His protection by repenting of our sin and believing the gospel. (Mark 1:15; 1 Corinthians 15:3-4; Romans 10:9; Ephesians 1:13-14, 19-20; 3:20)

- We protect ourselves from sin by living by faith in Jesus.

    - **Galatians 2:20** I have been **crucified with Christ**. It is no longer I who live, but **Christ who lives in me**. And the life **I now live in the flesh I live by faith in the Son of God**, who **loved me and gave himself for me.** (How to live by faith in Jesus: We attempt to obey the written word expecting Jesus to fulfill our attempt with His power.)

- Jesus gave us the written word and proved it was true. (2 Timothy 3:16; John 2:18-22)

- The written word directs us how to live without being destroyed by sin. (2 Timothy 3:16-17; Romans 12:2)

- Sin poisons our life. God's Word is the antidote for sin.

- The antidote is most effective when administered from birth by the family and by the local church. (Proverbs 6:20; Ephesians 6:1-4; 2 Timothy 1:5; 3:10-15)

- The antidote is most effective when taken at the best time of a person's day (not mixed with other activities) and meditated on throughout the day and night. (Joshua 1:8; Psalm 1:1-3)

- The antidote is most effective when hidden in the heart. (Psalm 119:11)

What we are to do with what we have heard from Scripture

- Recognize sin is our greatest danger, repent of our sin and believe the gospel.

- Make sure we know the danger of sin and how to protect ourselves.

- Daily spend our best time in the word and prayer, learning the Word of God formally and systematically.

- At every opportunity use the word of God to reprove, rebuke and encourage with great patience and instruction.

- Test yourself to see if you realize sin is your greatest danger: Do you have a desire to learn and live God's word? If not, then you don't see sin as your greatest danger. Are you protecting your family and those around you by helping them know Jesus, know His Word, the Bible, and helping them obey His Word by faith in Him? If not, you don't acknowledge sin is your greatest danger.

THE CHARACTERISTICS OF SIN

Discipline-Making Pathway

Preferred Future

Characteristics of Sin

Current Reality

Why it Matters: Knowing sin's characteristics reveals our own sin, our greatest danger.

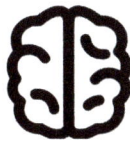

The Life Plan is an integrated whole to be lived out by faith each day until it is the lifestyle of the disciple-maker.

THE CHARACTERISTICS OF SIN

Facts on "Flesh" / "Sin Nature"

What do you want in your life?

Galatians 5:19-21 "Now the works of the flesh are evident: sexual immorality, impurity, sensuality, idolatry, sorcery, enmity, strife, jealousy, fits of anger, rivalries, dissensions, divisions, envy, drunkenness, orgies, and things like these. I warn you, as I warned you before, that those who do such things will not inherit the kingdom of God." ESV

OR

Galatians 5:22-23 "But the fruit of the Spirit is love, joy, peace, patience, kindness, goodness, faithfulness, gentleness, self-control..." ESV

Romans 5:12 Therefore, just as sin came into the world through one man, and death through sin, and so death spread to all men because all sinned...

Matthew 1:21 She will bear a son, and you shall call his name Jesus, for he will save his people from their sins.

Fact 1:

The flesh is weak: experiencing some incapacity or limitation, weak.

Romans 6:19 I put this in human terms because you are <u>weak</u> in your **natural selves**. Just as you used to offer the parts of your body in slavery to impurity and to ever-increasing wickedness, so now offer them in slavery to righteousness leading to holiness.

^NKJ **Romans 6:19** I speak in human *terms* because of the <u>weakness</u> of your **flesh**. For just as you presented your members *as* slaves of uncleanness, and of lawlessness *leading* to *more* lawlessness, so now present your members *as* slaves *of* righteousness for holiness.

Matthew 26:41 Watch and pray so that you will not fall into temptation. The spirit is willing, but the **body** is <u>weak</u>.

^NKJ **Matthew 26:41** Watch and pray, lest you enter into temptation. The spirit indeed *is* willing, but the **flesh** *is* <u>weak</u>.

Fact 2:

The flesh gives us passions that are sinful and pleasurable; that cause us to bite and devour one another when we should love one another. The passions cause us to do what God says not to do and not do what God says to do.

Romans 7:5 For when we were controlled by the **sinful nature,** {5 Or the flesh; also in verse 25} the <u>sinful passions</u> aroused by the law were at work in our bodies, so that we bore fruit for death.

^NKJ^ **Romans 7:5** For when we were in the **flesh**, the sinful passions which were aroused by the law were at work in our members to bear fruit to death.

Hebrews 11:25 He chose to be mistreated along with the people of God rather than to enjoy the pleasures of sin for a short time.

^NKJ^ **Hebrews 11:25** choosing rather to suffer affliction with the people of God than to enjoy the passing pleasures of sin,

Galatians 5:13-15 You, my brothers, were called to be free. But do not use your freedom to indulge **the sinful nature**; {*13* Or the flesh; also in verses 16, 17, 19 and 24} rather, serve one another in love. ¹⁴ The entire law is summed up in a single command: "Love your neighbor as yourself." {*14* Lev. 19:18} ¹⁵ If you keep on biting and devouring each other, watch out or you will be destroyed by each other.

^NKJ^ **Galatians 5:13-15** For you, brethren, have been called to liberty; only do not *use* liberty as an opportunity for **the flesh**, but through love serve one another. ¹⁴ For all the law is fulfilled in one word, *even* in this: "You shall love your neighbor as yourself." ¹⁵ But if you bite and devour one another, beware lest you be consumed by one another!

Fact 3:
Nothing good dwells in the flesh. Although we desire to do right we often don't do the right we desire to do, but we do the wrong thing.

Romans 7:18 I know that nothing good lives in me, that is, in my **sinful nature**. For I have the desire to do what is good, but I cannot carry it out.

^NKJ^ **Romans 7:18** For I know that in me (that is, in my **flesh**) nothing good dwells; for to will is present with me, but *how* to perform what is good I do not find.

Fact 4:
The flesh produces misery, deep distress, dissatisfaction, unhappiness and causes a wretched person to want to be rescued.

Romans 7:24 What a wretched man I am! Who will rescue me from this **body (somatos)** of death?

^NKJ^ **Romans 7:24** O wretched man that I am! Who will deliver me from this **body (somatos)** of death?

Fact 5:

The flesh enslaves non-believers to sin and deceived believers allow themselves to be enslaved to sin. The Christian is not a slave to sin, unless he/she submits as a slave to sin.

Romans 7:25 Thanks be to God-- through Jesus Christ our Lord! So then, I myself in my mind am a slave to God's law, but in the **sinful nature** a slave to the law of sin.

NKJ **Romans 7:25** I thank God -- through Jesus Christ our Lord! So then, with the mind I myself serve the law of God, but with the **flesh** the law of sin.

Hebrews 3:13 But encourage one another daily, as long as it is called Today, so that none of you may be hardened by sin's deceitfulness.

NKJ **Hebrews 3:13** but exhort one another daily, while it is called "Today," lest any of you be hardened through the deceitfulness of sin.

Romans 6:18 You have been set free from sin and have become slaves to righteousness.

NKJ **Romans 6:18** And having been set free from sin, you became slaves of righteousness.

Fact 6:

Futile thinking, darkened understanding, hardened heart, and callousness toward sin are characteristics of the flesh that the Christian is to no longer walk in.

Ephesians 2:1-3 As for you, you were dead in your transgressions and sins, ² in which you used to live when you followed the ways of this world and of the ruler of the kingdom of the air, the spirit who is now at work in those who are disobedient. ³ All of us also lived among them at one time, gratifying the cravings of our **sinful nature** {3 Or our flesh} and following **its** desires and thoughts. Like the rest, we were by nature objects of wrath.

NKJ **Ephesians 2:1-3** And you He made alive, who were dead in trespasses and sins, ² in which you once walked according to the course of this world, according to the prince of the power of the air, the spirit who now works in the sons of disobedience, ³ among whom also we all once conducted ourselves in the lusts of our **flesh**, fulfilling the desires of the **flesh** and of the mind, and were by nature children of wrath, just as the others.

Ephesians 4:17-19 So I tell you this, and insist on it in the Lord, that you must no longer live as the Gentiles do, in the futility of their thinking. ¹⁸ They are darkened in their understanding and separated from the life of God because of the ignorance that is in them due to the hardening of their hearts. ¹⁹ Having lost all sensitivity, they have given themselves over to sensuality so as to indulge in every kind of impurity, with a continual lust for more.

^NKJ^ **Ephesians 4:17-19** This I say, therefore, and testify in the Lord, that you should no longer walk as the rest of the Gentiles walk, in the futility of their mind, ¹⁸ having their understanding darkened, being alienated from the life of God, because of the ignorance that is in them, because of the blindness of their heart; ¹⁹ who, being past feeling, have given themselves over to lewdness, to work all uncleanness with greediness.

Fact 7:
The flesh wars against the soul seeking to get us to do what the Lord commands us not to do or not do what the Lord says to do.

1 Peter 2:11 Dear friends, I urge you, as aliens and strangers in the world, to abstain from **sinful desires**, which war against your soul.

^NKJ^ **1 Peter 2:11** Beloved, I beg you as sojourners and pilgrims, abstain from **fleshly lusts** which war against the soul,

Fact 8:
The flesh causes us to think sinfully, according to the ways of the world. (Romans 12:2a)

Romans 8:5 Those who live according to the **sinful nature** have their minds set on what that nature desires; but those who live in accordance with the Spirit have their minds set on what the Spirit desires.

^NKJ^ **Romans 8:5** For those who live according to the **flesh** set their minds on the things of the flesh, but those who live according to the Spirit, the things of the Spirit.

Fact 9:
The thinking of the mind of the flesh leads to death.

Romans 8:6 The mind of **sinful man** {6 Or mind set on the flesh} is death, but the mind controlled by the Spirit is life and peace;

^NKJ^ **Romans 8:6** For to be **carnally minded** is death, but to be spiritually minded is life and peace.

Fact 10:

The flesh won't and can't submit to God and cannot please God.

Romans 8:7-8 The **sinful mind** {7 Or the mind set on the flesh} is hostile to God. It does not submit to God's law, nor can it do so. ⁸ Those controlled by the sinful nature cannot please God.

^NKJ **Romans 8:7-8** Because the **carnal mind** is enmity against God; for it is not subject to the law of God, nor indeed can be. ⁸ So then, those who are in the flesh cannot please God.

Fact 11:

People without Christ are in the flesh and people in Christ can choose to live according to the flesh.

Romans 8:9 You, however, are controlled not by the **sinful nature** but by the Spirit, if the Spirit of God lives in you. And if anyone does not have the Spirit of Christ, he does not belong to Christ.

^NKJ **Romans 8:9** But you are not in the **flesh** but in the Spirit, if indeed the Spirit of God dwells in you. Now if anyone does not have the Spirit of Christ, he is not His.

1 Corinthians 3:1 Brothers, I could not address you as spiritual but as **worldly**-- mere infants in Christ.

^NKJ **1 Corinthians 3:1** And I, brethren, could not speak to you as to spiritual people but as to **carnal**, as to babes in Christ.

Fact 12:

People without Christ are obligated to live according to the flesh (sinful nature), and Christians are not obligated to obey the flesh, but can. People who obey the sin nature will die.

Romans 8:12-13 Therefore, brothers, we have an obligation-- but it is not to the **sinful nature**, to live according to it. ¹³ For if you live according to **the sinful nature**, you will die; but if by the Spirit you put to death the misdeeds of the body, you will live,

^NKJ **Romans 8:12-13** Therefore, brethren, we are debtors -- not to **the flesh**, to live according to the flesh. ¹³ For if you live according to **the flesh** you will die; but if by the Spirit you put to death the deeds of the body, you will live.

Lists of Sins of the Flesh:

Romans 1:24-32

Galatians 5:19-21

Ephesians 4:25-31

Colossians 3:5-9

1 Peter 2:1

Practical Exercise:

Spend some time reading through each passage listing each sin as you find it. Spend time confronting your own sin, prayerfully asking the Holy Spirit to shed light where darkness remains (1 John 1:5-10).

Romans 1:24-32

Galatians 5:19-21

Ephesians 4:25-31

Colossians 3:5-9

1 Peter 2:1

TRUE GRACE

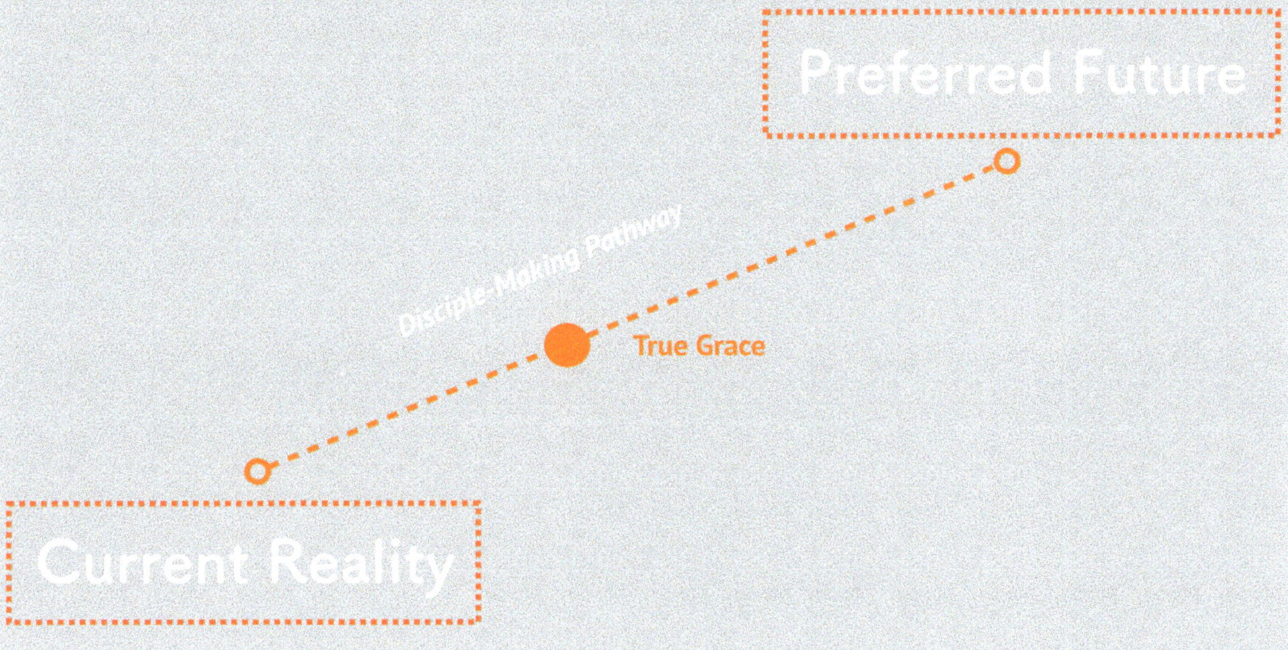

Why it Matters: Grace is every resource we are given to live eternally and abundantly.

The Life Plan is an integrated whole to be lived out by faith each day until it is the lifestyle of the disciple-maker.

TRUE GRACE

> **1 Peter 5:12**
>
> "With the help of Silas, whom I regard as a faithful brother, I have written to you briefly, encouraging you and testifying that this is the true grace of God. Stand fast in it."

God's Grace Removes the Penalty of Sin

Romans 6:23 For the wages of sin is death, but the free gift of God is eternal life in Christ Jesus our Lord.

Revelation 21:8 But as for the cowardly, the faithless, the detestable, as for murderers, the sexually immoral, sorcerers, idolaters, and all liars, their portion will be in the lake that burns with fire and sulfur, which is the second death.

Ephesians 2:8-9 For by grace you have been saved through faith. And this is not your own doing; it is the gift of God, ⁹ not a result of works, so that no one may boast.

Romans 5:1 Therefore, since we have been justified by faith, we have peace with God through our Lord Jesus Christ.

God's Grace Overcomes Sin's Power

2 Corinthians 12:9 But he said to me, "My grace is sufficient for you, for my power is made perfect in weakness." Therefore I will boast all the more gladly of my weaknesses, so that the power of Christ may rest upon me.

Galatians 2:20 I have been crucified with Christ. It is no longer I who live, but Christ who lives in me. And the life I now live in the flesh I live by faith in the Son of God, who loved me and gave himself for me.

Romans 6:6-7 We know that our old self was crucified with him in order that the body of sin might be brought to nothing, so that we would no longer be enslaved to sin. ⁷ For one who has died has been set free from sin.

Ephesians 1:13-14 In him you also, when you heard the word of truth, the gospel of your salvation, and believed in him, were sealed with the promised Holy Spirit, ¹⁴ who is the guarantee of our inheritance until we acquire possession of it, to the praise of his glory.

Ephesians 1:19 and what is the surpassing greatness of His power toward us who believe.

Ephesians 3:20 Now to him who is able to do far more abundantly than all that we ask or think, according to the power at work within us,

God's Grace Equips Us to Serve One Another

1 Peter 4:10 As each has received a gift, use it to serve one another, as good stewards of God's varied grace.

Galatians 2:20 I have been crucified with Christ. It is no longer I who live, but Christ who lives in me. And the life I now live in the flesh I live by faith in the Son of God, who loved me and gave himself for me.

1 Corinthians 15:10 But by the grace of God I am what I am, and his grace toward me was not in vain. On the contrary, I worked harder than any of them, though it was not I, but the grace of God that is with me.

Romans 12:3 For by the grace given to me I say to everyone among you not to think of himself more highly than he ought to think, but to think with sober judgment, each according to the measure of faith that God has assigned.

True Grace ✠

Grace = the unmerited favor of God

GRACE to be Saved 1

God's Grace Removes the Penalty of Sin

Ephesians 2:8-9

Romans 6:23

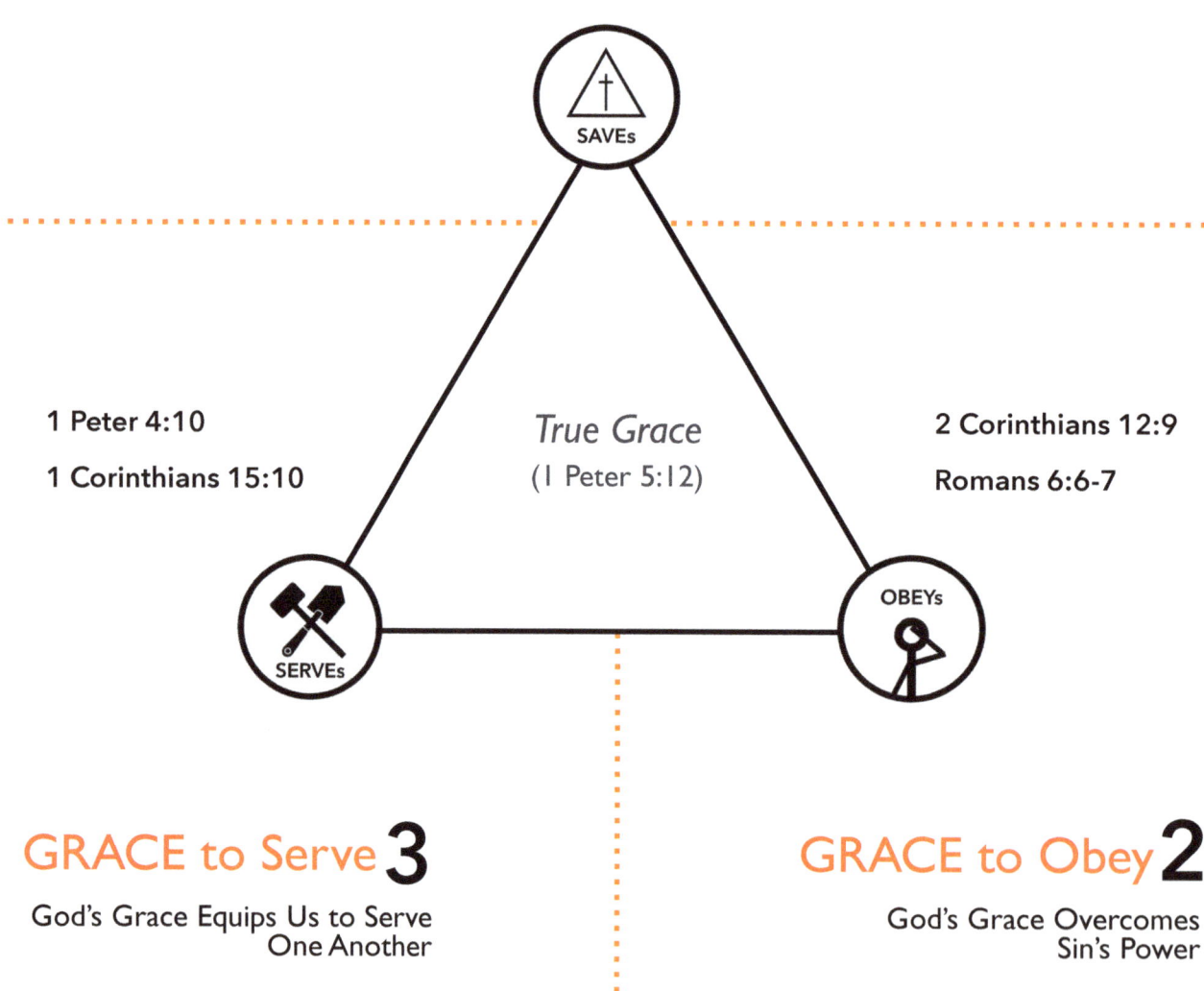

1 Peter 4:10

1 Corinthians 15:10

True Grace
(1 Peter 5:12)

2 Corinthians 12:9

Romans 6:6-7

GRACE to Serve 3

God's Grace Equips Us to Serve One Another

GRACE to Obey 2

God's Grace Overcomes Sin's Power

PART 2

the Disciple-Maker
Preferred Future

WE ARE STATEMENTS

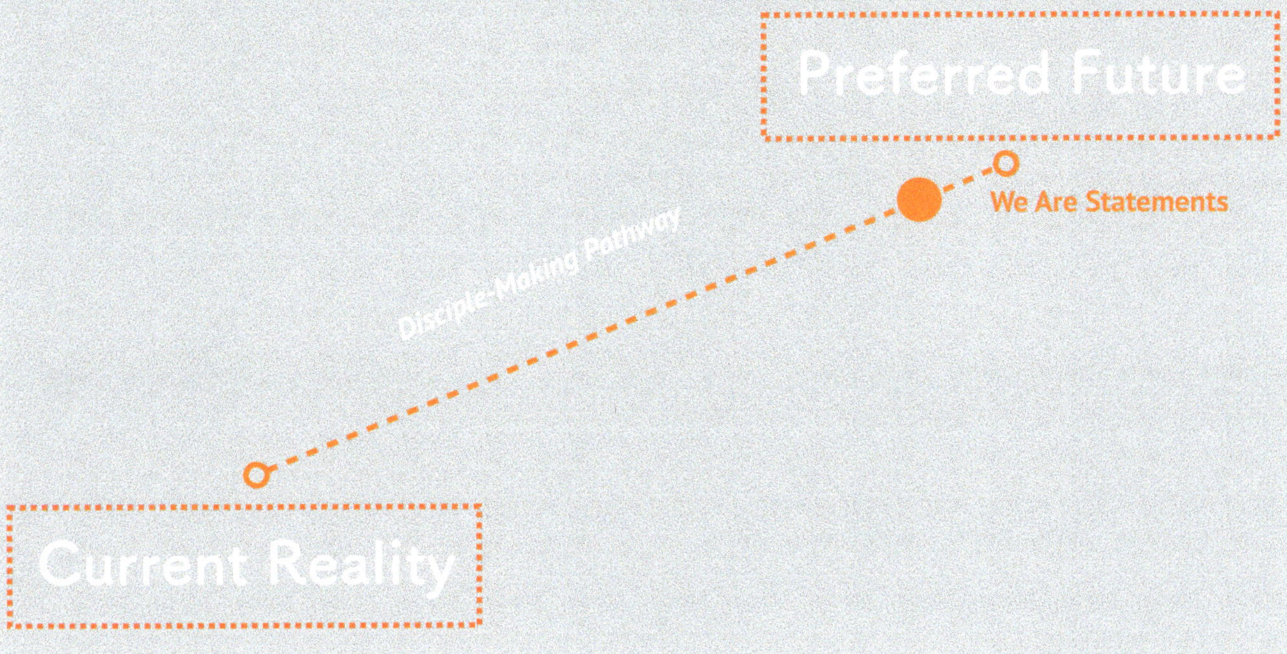

[Diagram: Disciple-Making Pathway from Current Reality to Preferred Future, with "We Are Statements" marked near the Preferred Future end.]

Why it Matters: These are how we live out the life and mission of Jesus.

The Life Plan is an integrated whole to be lived out by faith each day until it is the lifestyle of the disciple-maker.

1) WE ARE

Training Disciple-Makers

Matthew 28:19-20

"Go therefore and **make disciples** of all nations, **baptizing** them in the name of the Father and of the Son and of the Holy Spirit, **teaching** them to observe all that I have commanded you. And behold, I am with you always, to the end of the age."

What does the grammar tell us about this passage in Matthew's Gospel? The main verb is **"make disciples."** It describes action to be done in its entirety as a person walks through life (Matt 10:6; Rom 15:20-21). The process of disciple-making is broken down into three parts.

The first is evangelism. This is simply sharing the life and truth of Jesus with people of all nations, revealing their need to repent and believe the gospel.

The second is baptism. A person is baptized after they have repented and believed the gospel.

The third part is about teaching the new disciple to persistently obey everything Jesus Christ commanded.

At Plethos, the Life Plan offers every disciple-maker a platform for growth and maturity through obedience to Christ. What we call **The Big Three Keystone Habits** are an essential part of the training process:

1. Systematic reading of the Bible and having a way to hold yourself accountable to practice what you learn each day.

2. Learning and applying Galatians 2:20 *(Living the Life of Christ)*.

3. Passing on what you are learning in your home and / or circle of influence.

Jesus goes on to promise his presence through the entire disciple-making process, from salvation to baptism on through maturity. As we disciple others in the love and truth of Jesus, He is with us.

Our mission is to train faithful men and women to be disciple-makers in their home and circle of influence. We do this in four key areas of life: the family (Deut 4:9; Deut 6:4-9), one man teaching faithful men (2 Tim 2:2), one woman teaching faithful women (Titus 2:3-5), and within the local church (2 Tim 3:14 - 4:5; Acts 20:27-28).

We believe the job of making disciples is for every believer and Plethos is committed to training disciple-makers worldwide.

2 WE ARE

Helping Disciples to Train in Godliness

1 Timothy 4:7-8

Have nothing to do with irreverent, silly myths. Rather train yourself for godliness; for while bodily training is of some value, godliness is of value in every way, as it holds promise for the present life and also for the life to come.

Greek Lesson

γυμνάζω; **verb** [γυμνασία, ας, ἡ; **noun, 'physical exercise, bodily training'**] **train, discipline,** in NT only by extension of the physical aspect, **1 Timothy 4:7-8;** Hebrews 5:14; 12:11; 2 Peter 2:14. (Note: The verb "train" is used in verse 7 and the noun "training" is used in verse 8.) Train, is a command for a person to spend his entire life training in godliness.

εὐσέβεια, ας, ἡ *piety,* **godliness,** *religion* Ac 3:12; 1 Ti 2:2; 3:16; 2 Ti 3:5; Tit 1:1. Godliness is being like Christ and doing Christ's work (1 Corinthians 11:1). Every disciple has the capacity to learn the word of God and live the word of God (Gal 2:20). Our role is to help followers of Jesus discover their capacity to train in godliness.

Training in godliness, or, living like Christ, is intentional and multifaceted. It's teaching disciples:

1. How to eliminate the ways of the world from their life (1 Tim 4:7a; Rom 12:2a).

2. How to avoid untruth by learning and living the truth, the word of God (John 17:17; 2 Timothy 3:16).

3. To daily, systematically read the Bible and have personal accountability to practice what you learn.

When a disciple obeys the written word of God they are transformed over their lifetime in godliness (Rom 12:2b).

We train every disciple to know it is not enough to merely gain *head knowledge*, but to grow in *experiential knowledge* of God's word. Likewise it is not enough to merely gain a *head knowledge* of God's power, we know that *experiential knowledge* is key to growing in godliness. Our desire is to help every disciple learn to obey God's word by faith in Jesus so that they will experience the power of God in the scriptures. Let's not become like the Pharisees who had a head knowledge of God's word and power, but lived in sin because they did not live by faith in the Son of God (Matt 22:29; 23:2-3; Rom 9:30-32).

Our hope is to motivate disciples to train in godliness by teaching the value of godliness (1 Tim 4:8). A lifestyle of godliness will cause each of us to experience an abundant and eternal life (John 10:10b).

Continued Study: See the following documents to help train a disciple in godliness:

1. Living the Life of Christ

2. Matthew 6:33 Practice

3. How to Study the Bible

4. The Student, the Fish and Agassiz

3 WE ARE

Helping Each Family Unit be a Love and Truth Center

Love & Truth

"A new command I give you: **Love** one another. As I have loved you, so you must love one another. By this all men will **know** that you are my disciples, if you love one another." **John 13:34-35**

So Jesus said to the Jews who had believed him, "If you abide in my word, you are truly my disciples, and you will know the truth, and the the truth will set you free." **John 8:31-32**

At Plethos, our desire is to help every disciple transform their home and local church into a love and truth center. What is a love and truth center? It is a hospitable environment where the love and truth of Christ are lived and shared. As Peter instructs, we're called to purify our souls by obedience to the truth so we can love one another earnestly from the heart (1 Pet 1:22).

Disciples are commanded to do everything in love (1 Cor 16:14). In 1 Corinthians 13:4-8a Paul gives us sixteen action words that describe expressions of love. In Hebrews 12:5-6 we're told that God disciplines out of love. Think about how encouraging our homes and local churches would be with this type of divine love expressed.

Our families are not only to be centers for experiencing God's love, but His truth as well. We must know the truth in order to be a love and truth center. What is truth? John 17:17 tells us that God's Word is truth. The best way to get to know the truth is to be in the Word; to daily, systematically read through the Bible and hold ourselves accountable to practice what we learn. This takes hard work (Prov 2:1-4; 2 Tim 2:15).

Ultimately, we practice being a love and truth center when we obey what Jesus taught His disciples who then passed on His love and truth. When you and I learn and live out Galatians 2:20 and Matthew 6:33 we are fostering healthy love and truth centers in our homes and local churches.

A great picture of a love and truth center is found in Galatians 5:22-23. On the other hand, a picture of a sin center is found in Galatians 5:19-20. Read through these and ask yourself, "Is my home a love and truth center or a sin center?" Put that another way, "Which kind of center is my home most often?"

Continued Study:

1. Matthew 28:19-20
2. Matthew 6:33
3. Galatians 2:20

THE LOVE & TRUTH CENTER

A Self-Assessment Tool for Christians
WE ARE #3

HIGH LOVE

(I feel I am like Christ)

Enabler: Tolerant

Tolerates sin to another's destruction.

Lamentations 2:14
1 Corinthians 5:1-5

(I am like Christ)

Christlike: Filled by the Spirit, Empowered by the Gospel

Displays love and truth daily.

Galatians 5:22-23
Ephesians 4:15

Heart +
Soul −
Mind −
Body +

Heart +
Soul +
Mind +
Body +

LOW TRUTH

HIGH TRUTH

Heart −
Soul −
Mind −
Body −

Heart −
Soul −
Mind +
Body +

(I am not like Christ)

Worldly: Apathetic

Confesses Christ, but lives conformed to the world.

1 Corinthians 3:1-3
2 Corinthians 13:5

(I think I am like Christ)

Legalist: Prideful, Critical

Trying to live by their own power and expecting others to do the same.

Galatians 3:3
Colossians 2:23

LOW LOVE

4 WE ARE

Distributing the Grace of God by Serving One Another

1 Peter 4:10

As each has received a gift, use it to serve one another, as good stewards of God's varied grace.

The Greek words translated **"gift"** and **"grace"** have the same root. Digging in we discover that *gift* is an expression of divine *grace*. As Christians, when we use our particular gift of grace to serve others, we are distributing the particular resource God has given to one of His people in need. As a result, we build one another up in love (Eph 4:15-16).

Jesus instructed His people, "More happiness (blessing) is gained by giving than it is by receiving" (Acts 20:35b). When we realize that the way to happiness is giving, our desire and motivation to give will increase. But, we must also humbly receive what is given to us. The Body of Christ is most happy, whole, and effective in accomplishing God's will when His gifts of grace are both given and received.

By design, the Lord has distributed His grace gifts to each individual part of His Body, the Church (1 Cor 12:4-31). Paul wrote that Apostles, Prophets, Evangelists, Pastors, and Teachers are to restore the Body to do God's work in the church and the world (Eph 4:11-12). The word often translated as "equip, prepare, or train" could best be translated "restore." People sick with sin are in no condition to serve. The role of the disciple, full of God's gift of grace, is to restore others to spiritual health so they can effectively serve the Body using God's gifts.

Gifts of Grace

- Romans 12:6-8
- 1 Corinthians 12:8-11, 28-30
- 1 Peter 4:10-11
- Ephesians 4:11

It's important to remember that the Holy Spirit distributes the gifts to His people as He wills (1 Cor 12:11). At Plethos we earnestly desire that each local Body of Christ be filled with all of His gifts. Psalm 37:4 says that when we delight in the Lord, He will give us the desires of our heart. Paul notes in Philippians 2:13 how God is at work in each believer to will and to do His good pleasure.

When we desire and distribute the grace of God to the people of God our home as well as our local church will become love and truth centers. Then, each disciple will become effective at fulfilling God's primary mission in their community to seek and save the lost (Luke 19:10; Matt 28:19-20).

We are never more like Jesus than when we *give*, *serve* and humbly *receive*.

5 WE ARE

Families on Mission

Deuteronomy 6:4-9

"Hear, O Israel: The LORD our God, the LORD is one. *(All adults and children)* You shall love the LORD your God with all your heart and with all your soul and with all your might. *(All adults and children)* And these words that I command you today shall be on your heart. *(All parents)* You shall teach them diligently to your children, and shall talk of them when you sit in your house, and when you walk by the way, and when you lie down, and when you rise. *(All parents)* You shall bind them as a sign on your hand, and they shall be as frontlets between your eyes. *(All parents)* You shall write them on the doorposts of your house and on your gates.

The **primary place** where disciple-making takes place is given in Deuteronomy 6:4-9, the family. The following passages affirm and give direction for the primary way of passing on the faith to the next generation.

Ephesians 6:1-4 *"Children, **obey your parents** in the Lord, for this is right. 2 '**Honor your father and mother** (this is the first commandment with a promise), 3 that it may go well with you and that you may live long in the land.' 4 **Fathers**, do not provoke your children to anger, but **bring them up in the discipline and instruction of the Lord.**"*

Proverbs 6:20 *"My son, **keep your father's commandment**, and **forsake not your mother's teaching**."*

Within the primary place, the family, we engage our primary assignment through the lens of the Life Plan. What is our primary assignment?

At Plethos we believe our **primary assignment** for the basic unit of any culture, the family, is the Great Commission (the Great Assignment) given by our Lord Jesus Christ, *"Go therefore and make disciples of all nations, baptizing them in the name of the Father and of the Son and of the Holy Spirit, teaching them to observe all that I have commanded you. And behold, I am with you always, to the end of the age."* (Matt. 28:19-20 ESV)

The Life Plan, then, is the foundational and focused tool designed to help each parent fulfill their primary assignment in their primary place. In particular, the **Disciple-Maker Preferred Future** proclaims the six 'We Are Statements' every member of the family is encouraged to aim for in order to live out the Great Commission and become a family on mission.

Proverbs 6:20 My son, **keep your father's commandment**, and **forsake not your mother's teaching**.

The **Disciple-Maker Pathway** offers guidance to families growing in the Disciple-Maker Preferred Future. This pathway, made up of six discipleship tools found in the Life Plan, is to be taught in the home by the parent(s) through daily, memorable, and repetitive formal and informal instruction and example. We believe as families grow in Christ, so does their mission.

6 WE ARE

Teaching the Consequences of Not Obeying Jesus

Luke 6:46-49

"Why do you call me 'Lord, Lord,' and not do what I tell you? Everyone who comes to me and hears my words and does them, I will show you what he is like: he is like a man building a house, who dug deep and laid the foundation on the rock. And when a flood arose, the stream broke against that house and could not shake it, because it had been well built. **But the one who hears and does not do them** is like a man who built a house on the ground without a foundation. When the stream broke against it, immediately it fell, and the ruin of that house was great."

Jesus' Key Question: *"Why do you call me 'Lord, Lord,' and not do what I tell you?"*

Jesus is asking people to think through the importance of obeying His teaching. Disciples are to imitate Jesus and ask those we disciple, and those in our circle of influence, this very question.

Think about this: If we build our house on a firm foundation it will not be ruined when a flood rises up. The rock foundation would not be shaken. However, if we build our house on the dirt with no foundation, it will inevitably be ruined in a flood. Disciples who obey the commands of Jesus will stand firm when confronted by the storms and floods of sin. However, the one who does not obey Jesus' commands will be ruined.

Reading through the Bible we see that God continually presses this point. Proverbs 4:18-19 is a good example, *"But the **path of the righteous** (obedience) is like the light of dawn, which shines brighter and brighter until full day. ¹⁹ The **way of the wicked** (disobedience) is like deep darkness; they do not know over what they stumble."*

Revelation 7:2-3 demonstrates the same principle. The servant of God (obedient disciple) is sealed from the harm coming as judgment of sin, but the disobedient person will get the full measure of harm. *"Then I saw another angel ascending from the rising of the sun, with the seal of the living God, and he called with a loud voice to the four angels who had been given power to harm earth and sea, saying, 'Do not harm the earth or the sea or the trees, until we have sealed the servants of our God on their foreheads.'"*

As disciples, you and I are to be informing others of the consequences of sinful living and the blessings of righteous living. Both realities of the Gospel are necessary for raising up honest and healthy disciples who will make disciples. Prudence dwells with wisdom. **Prudence is knowing the future results of your present actions (Proverbs 22:3).** Knowing the consequences for not obeying Jesus is key to being prudent. When someone knows the consequences it helps them make wise decisions.

Our desire at Plethos is to help equip disciple-makers with the discernment necessary to profess the many blessings of Christ as well as the consequences of sin.

PART 3
the Disciple-Maker Pathway

LIVING THE LIFE OF CHRIST

Disciple-Making Pathway

- Current Reality
- Living the Life of Christ
- Preferred Future

Why it Matters: This is how we live a victorious Christian life in the midst of any circumstance.

The Life Plan is an integrated whole to be lived out by faith each day until it is the lifestyle of the disciple-maker.

LIVING THE LIFE OF CHRIST

Galatians 2:20

Galatians 2:20

"I have been crucified with Christ. It is no longer I who live, but Christ who lives in me. And the life I now live in the flesh I live by faith in the Son of God, who loved me and gave himself for me."

Greek Lesson

"I have been crucified with" (συνεσταύρωμαι):

verb indicative mood (fact) perfect tense (completed in the past and remains complete in the present) passive voice (subject is acted on by an outside force, in this case, God) 1st person singular.

Part 1 / OUR VICTORY
"I have been crucified with Christ."

What does it mean to be crucified with Christ? (This happens when we repent of our sins and believe the gospel.)

Romans 5:10 For if while we were enemies we were reconciled to God by the death of his Son, much more, now that we are reconciled, shall we be saved by his life. **(Free from the penalty of sin - Justification)**

Romans 6:6-7 We know that our old self was crucified with him in order that the body of sin might be brought to nothing (Greek "rendered powerless"), so that we would no longer be enslaved to sin. ⁷ For one who has died has been set free from sin. **(Free from the power of sin - Sanctification)**

John 14:1-3 "Let not your hearts be troubled. Believe in God; believe also in me. ² In my Father's house are many rooms. If it were not so, would I have told you that I go to prepare a place for you? ³ And if I go and prepare a place for you, I will come again and will take you to myself, that where I am you may be also." **(Free from the presence of sin - Glorification)**

Hebrews 2:14-15 Since therefore the children share in flesh and blood, he himself likewise partook of the same things, that through death he might destroy (Greek "rendered powerless") the one who has the power of death, that is, the devil, ¹⁵ and deliver all those who through fear of death were subject to lifelong slavery. **(Free from the Power of Satan)**

FACT Anyone who repents of their sins and believes the gospel has been freed from the penalty, power, and, one day, the presence of sin; and freed from the power of Satan.

Part 2 / OUR RESOURCE
"It is no longer I who live, but Christ who lives in me."

What does it mean to have Christ living in me?

Romans 8:9-11 You, however, are not in the flesh but in **the Spirit**, if in fact the **Spirit of God** dwells in you. Anyone who does not have **the Spirit of Christ** does not belong to him. [10] But **if Christ** is in you, although the body is dead because of sin, **the Spirit** is life because of righteousness. [11] If **the Spirit** of him who raised Jesus from the dead dwells in you, he who raised Christ Jesus from the dead will also give life to your mortal bodies through **his Spirit who dwells in you**. (The trinity is one God who lives in each believer).

Matthew 28:19-20 Go therefore and make disciples of all nations, baptizing them in the name (singular noun) of the Father and of the Son and of the Holy Spirit[20] teaching them to observe all that I have commanded you. And behold, I am with you always, to the end of the age.

The Father, Son, and Holy Spirit are one God**.**

Luke 1:37 For nothing **is impossible with God**.

> **FACT** Nothing God commands a believer to do is impossible for that believer to do.

Part 3 / OUR ACCESS
"And the life I now live in the flesh I live by faith in the Son of God"

How do we daily live by faith? How does living by faith in the Son of God benefit us?

2 Thessalonians 1:11 To this end we always pray for you, **that our God** may make you worthy of his calling and **may fulfill** every resolve for good and **every work of faith by his power**,

Ephesians 1:19-20 and what is the immeasurable greatness of his power toward us who believe, according to the working of his great might [20] that he worked in Christ when he raised him from the dead (resurrection power) and seated him at his right hand in the heavenly places,

Ephesians 3:20 Now to him who is able to do far more abundantly than all that we ask or think, according to the power at work within us,

> **FACT** We can access all the resources of Christ by faith in Him. Faith is attempting to obey the Lord expecting Him to fulfill our attempt with His power that works within the believer.

Part 4 / OUR MOTIVATION
"who loved me and gave himself for me."

How great is the love of Jesus?

Love Did: Romans 5:8 but God shows his love for us in that while we were still sinners, Christ died for us.

Love Does: John 15:13 Greater love has no one than this, that someone lays down his life for his friends.

Love Is: 1 Corinthians 13:4-8a Love is patient, love is kind. It does not envy, it does not boast, it is not proud. [5] It is not rude, it is not self-seeking, it is not easily angered, it keeps no record of wrongs. [6] Love does not delight in evil but rejoices with the truth. [7] It always protects, always trusts, always hopes, always perseveres. [8] Love never fails.

> **FACT** Jesus loves us with the greatest love of all and His love never fails.

1. VICTORY

"I have been crucified with Christ"

What does it mean to be crucified with Christ?

FREE from the 4 P's:
- **Penalty** of sin (Romans 5:10)
- **Power** of sin (Romans 6:6-7)
- **Presence** of sin (John 14:1-3)
- **Power** of Satan (Hebrews 2:14-15)

FACT / Anyone who repents of their sins and believes the gospel has been freed from the penalty, power and presence of sin; freed from the Power of Satan.

2. RESOURCE

"It is no longer I who live, but Christ who lives in me"

What does it mean to have Christ living in me?

1. The Trinity is One God who **lives in** each believer (Ex. Romans 8:9-11)
2. Our **Resource**, Father, Son & Spirit, are One God (Matthew 28:19-20, singular noun)
3. God is our **Resource** who can accomplish the impossible (Luke 1:37)

FACT / Nothing God commands a believer to do is impossible for that believer to do.

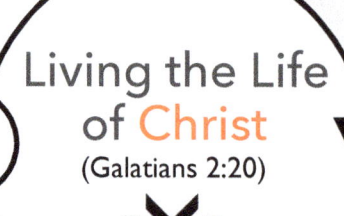

Living the Life of Christ
(Galatians 2:20)

4. MOTIVATION

"Who loved me and gave Himself for me."

How great is the love of Jesus?

Motivated to Grow & Multiply because:
- *Love Did:* Christ's death (Romans 5:8)
- *Love Does:* Christ's sacrifice (John 15:13)
- *Love Is:* Christ's actions (1 Corinthians 13:4-8a)

FACT / Jesus loves us with the greatest love of all and His love never fails.

3. ACCESS

"And the life I now live in the flesh I live by faith in the Son of God"

How do we live by faith?

1. Power **through faith** (2 Thessalonians 1:11)
2. Resurrection Power **through belief** (Ephesians 1:19-20)
3. Unimaginable Power **at work** within us (Ephesians 3:20)

FACT / We can access all the resources of Christ by faith in Him. Faith is attempting to obey the Lord expecting Him to fulfill our attempt with His power that works within the believer.

MATTHEW 6:33 PRACTICE

Diagram: Disciple-Making Pathway from Current Reality to Preferred Future, with M6:33 Practice marked along the path.

Why it Matters: It causes us to continually pursue God's rule and righteousness knowing we will have everything we need to live an abundant life in Christ.

The Life Plan is an integrated whole to be lived out by faith each day until it is the lifestyle of the disciple-maker.

MATTHEW 6:33 PRACTICE

Matthew 6:33

"But seek first the kingdom of God and his righteousness, and all these things will be added to you."

The Matthew 6:33 Practice is obeying the commands, the instruction of Jesus, 24/7 in every area of our life. This results in healthy Gal. 5:22-23 relationships, fruitful Jn. 15:5 lives, the security of certain material provision and protection from the evil one.

M6:33 Purpose: We need to do Matthew 6:33 Practice in every area of our life to achieve the "We Are…" statements of the Life Plan.

	Title Track 1	=	Parallel Track 2	=	Parallel Track 3
M6:33 PARALLEL EXAMPLES	SEEK ▶		▲ OBEY		▼ ABIDE ▲
TEXT	Matthew 6:33		Matthew 28:20 Romans 6:16		John 15:5 1 John 3:24
CONTEXT	*seeking* God's **kingdom** & **righteousness** is the lifelong practice of abiding in Christ and obeying His commands		*obedience* to Christ's commands in every area of life leads to a righteous pursuit of abiding in God		*abiding* in Christ is the overflow of the obedient pursuit of His commands and results in fruitful living

RESULTS

1. **Provision:**
    A. Specific: "All these things"
    B. General: "All these things"
2. **Protection:**
    A. Divine Protection: 2 Corinthians 10:4-5
    B. Divine Resistance: James 4:7
3. **Producing Fruit:** 'karpos' (gk)
    A. Saved souls: Romans 1:13 - *karpos* = "harvest"
    B. Help for people in need: Romans 15:28 - *karpos* = "what has been collected"
    C. Healthy lives / relationships: Galatians 5:22-23 - *karpos* = "fruit"
4. **Intimacy with Jesus:** John 14:21, 23

BIG IDEA

Practice obeying God's commands in every area of your life.

Title M6:33 Track 1: Seek

Matthew 6:33 "But seek first his kingdom and his righteousness, and all these things will be added to you."

Definition of "seek": Seek means to **pursue** something. The Greek grammar **commands** us to pursue continuously the Kingdom of God and His righteousness as a lifestyle.

Definition of "kingdom": The primary meaning of kingdom is **"the sovereign rule of a king"**. God is the King of kings.

Definition of "righteousness": Righteousness is the condition of being in right relationship with God, that is, free from sin. Sin is being or doing what God says not to be or do (Romans 7:16-20) or not being or doing what God says to do (James 4:17). We are made righteous (justified) by repenting of our sins and believing the gospel (Romans 4:20-25). We live righteously by obeying the commands (instruction) of Jesus (Romans 6:16b; Matthew 28:20).

When we seek first the Kingdom of God and His righteousness, we are learning and obeying the commands of Christ. **Matthew 6:33 Practice** is learning and obeying the commands of Christ in every area of our life (Matthew 28:20).

Parallel Track 2: Obey

Track 2: Obey offers the same insight as the M6:33 title track, *Seek*. We call this a parallel track in that the focus on *obedience* to God's commands offers the same results as M6:33. This can be taught as a stand-alone M6:33 tool or a correlating track to supplement the others.

Matthew 28:20 "…teaching them to observe all that I have commanded you. And behold, I am with you always, to the end of the age."

Romans 6:16 Do you not know that if you present yourselves to anyone as obedient slaves, you are slaves of the one whom you obey, either of sin, which leads to death, or of obedience, which leads to righteousness?

1. **Obedience** is a sign of the Spirit within us:

A. **Ezekiel 36:27** "And I will put my Spirit within you, and cause you to walk in my statutes and be careful to obey my rules."

B. **Ephesians 1:13** And you also were included in Christ when you heard the word of truth, the gospel of your salvation. Having **believed**, you were marked in him with a seal, the promised **Holy Spirit**…

2. **Obedience** expresses love to people and God:

    A. **1 John 5:2** By this we know that we love the children of God, when we love God and obey His commandments.

    B. **1 John 5:3** This is love for God: to obey His commands.

Parallel Track 3: Abide

Track 3: Abide offers the same insight as the M6:33 title track, *Seek*. We call this a parallel track in that the focus on *abiding* in Christ and His commands offers the same results as M6:33. This, too, can be taught as a stand-alone M6:33 tool or a correlating track to supplement the others.

John 15:5 "I am the vine; you are the branches. Whoever **abides** (English translation of Greek word "meno") in me and I in him, he it is that bears much fruit, for apart from me you can do nothing."

1 John 3:24 "Whoever keeps his commandments **abides** (English translation of Greek word "meno") in God, and God in him. And by this we know that he **abides** (English translation of Greek word "meno") in us, by the Spirit whom he has given us."

Definition of "abide": The general meaning of **abide** (meno) is to remain, dwell. We abide in the Lord by obeying God's commands.

To Seek, Obey & Abide All Result in:

1. **Provision** - "all these things" (Matthew 6:33b)

   A. **Specifically** in Matthew 6:33 refers to the things mentioned in Matthew 6:25, food and clothing or our material needs.

   B. **Generally** in Matthew 6:33 refers to everything we need to live a godly, fruitful life in our homes, work places, ministry sites, school, neighborhood, etc., and how to be protected from our spiritual enemies.

2. **Protection**

   A. **Divine protection** For the weapons of our warfare are not of the flesh but have divine power to destroy strongholds. 5 We destroy arguments and every lofty opinion raised against the knowledge of God, and take every thought captive to obey Christ (2 Corinthians 10:4-5).

   B. **Divine resistance** (We submit by obeying the Lord.) Submit yourselves therefore to God. Resist the devil, and he will flee from you (James 4:7).

3. **Producing Fruit**

   A. **The fruit of saved souls** I do not want you to be unaware, brothers, that I have often intended to come to you (but thus far have been prevented), in order that I may reap some **harvest** (English translation of Greek word **karpos**) among you as well as among the rest of the Gentiles (Romans 1:13).

   B. **The fruit of material aid for people in need** When therefore I have completed this and have delivered to them **what has been collected** (English translation of the Greek word **karpos**), I will leave for Spain by way of you (Romans 15:28).

   C. **The fruit of the Spirit in healthy relationships** But the **fruit** (English translation of Greek word **karpos**) of the Spirit is love, joy, peace, patience, kindness, goodness, faithfulness, 23 gentleness, self-control; against such things there is no law (Galatians 5:22-23).

4. **Intimacy with Jesus**

    A. **John 14:21, 23** "Whoever has my commandments and keeps them, he it is who loves me. And he who loves me will be loved by my Father, and I will love him and manifest myself to him." 23 Jesus answered him, "If anyone loves me, he will keep my word, and my Father will love him, and we will come to him and make our home with him."

Big Idea:

Practice obeying God's commands in every area of your life.

Examples of a Matthew 6:33 Life

Jesus Christ instructs us to express "honor" to the following people and the institution of marriage. Honor means to treat with high value.

- Honor the Lord – Revelation 5:13

- Honor mother and father – Matthew 15:4

- Honor elders who rule well – 1 Timothy 5:17; honor rulers – 1 Peter 2:17

- Husbands are to honor their wife – 1 Peter 3:7

- Honor everyone – 1 Peter 2:17

- Honor marriage – Hebrews 13:4

SYSTEMATIC READING OF THE BIBLE

Preferred Future

Disciple-Making Pathway

Sys. Reading of the Bible

Current Reality

Why it Matters: It provides renewal of the mind which leads to a transformed life. How we think shapes the way we live.

The Life Plan is an integrated whole to be lived out by faith each day until it is the lifestyle of the disciple-maker.

BIBLE READING PLAN

Keystone Habit #1

Grow in Your Ability to Understand

You can only understand God's Word if you have a proper relationship with Jesus.

As you read, let the Holy Spirit teach you God's thoughts (1 Cor 2:11-14; Eph 1:13-14). Each time you open your Bible confess your sins and ask God to guide you (Ps 66:18; Ps 119:33-40).

Bible Reading Plan for all Disciple-Makers

Begin with a proper mindset. Pray.

We recommend a daily reading rhythm that carries you systematically through the Word and a way to hold yourself accountable to practice what you read.

Read to learn and understand. If on some days you can't get through all the reading, then pick-up where you left off the day before. The goal is to spend time with the Lord while learning the Bible, not simply to get through it in a particular time period.

To aid application answer these three key Q's:

1. How am I to daily live?
2. How am I daily living?
3. What changes or growth do I need to make?

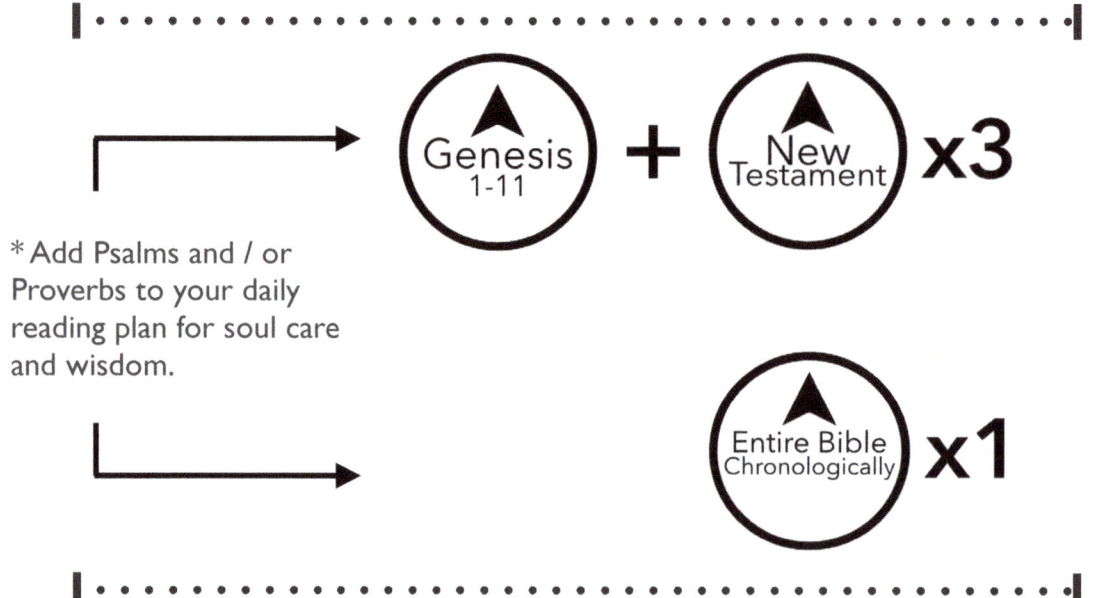

*Add Psalms and / or Proverbs to your daily reading plan for soul care and wisdom.

HOW TO STUDY THE BIBLE

Take Your Bible Studies Deeper

Gain the Ability to Understand

You can only understand God's Word if you have a proper relationship with Jesus.

When you are spiritually born again, the Holy Spirit will teach you God's thoughts (I Cor 2:12-14; Eph 1:13-14). Each time you open your Bible, though, you should confess your sins and ask God to guide you (Ps 66:18; Ps 119:33-40).

Our Motivation to Study

A. **Knowing that sin is the greatest danger** spurs us on toward life and truth in Christ through the Scriptures.

B. **Knowing a Galatians 2:20** kind of love spurs us on to know the source of that love.

Begin With a Proper Mindset

A. **Believe that the Bible is God's Word.** It is inspired by God and therefore without error; it never contradicts itself. In it, God reveals himself, his works, and his requirements. Through it the Holy Spirit guides, convicts, comforts, and strengthens us so that we will experience the fullness of God that comes from obedience. We must, therefore, submit ourselves to obey the Bible quickly and diligently.

B. **Understand your position in Christ.** You should study the Bible, not to be accepted by God, but rather so that you can get to know him and his will for you. If you are in Christ, you are already fully accepted and loved by God; he will not reject you because you miss a day of Bible reading.

C. **Embrace the value of Bible study.** Intently looking into the Word of God and obeying it brings blessing, guards against sin, protects your life, guides you in God's will, and builds you up so that you will be thoroughly equipped for every good work. (Jam 1:22-25; Ps 119:1,2,9,11,72,105; 2 Tim 3:16; Ps 1:1-3; Matt 4:4; John 6:68)

Bible study will help you experience life transformation that will conform you to God's good (gratifying), pleasing (satisfying), and perfect (completing) will—see Romans 12:2. God's Word will restore you and keep you from corruption (2 Pet 1:3-4; Eph 4:20-24). It will help you live life to the full both here and after you die (John 6:68; 10:10b). It will also teach you prudence, which means knowing the future results of your present actions (Prov 22:3).

D. **Recognize the difficulty.** You must search the Scriptures as if you were hunting for hidden treasure (Prov 2:1-5). It is hard work. You will face fatigue, opposition from the enemy, and frustration. But the treasure of knowing God is worth the effort.

E. **Long to know and glorify God.** Crave God's Word and guard against a "ho-hum" callousness toward spiritual things. (1 Pet 2:2-3; Heb 5:11)

Use a System for Reading

Strive to gain the whole counsel of God (Acts 20:27) by organizing your Bible reading according to the following suggestions:

A. **Specify a place** for studying the Bible. Being physically settled with available study tools on hand keeps us focused and prepared to dig into the Word.

B. **Specify a time** for studying the Bible. A regularly scheduled time for digging deeper into the Text fosters great personal accountability and greater fruitfulness in your studies.

C. **Read systematically** (i.e., in an organized way - see Bible Reading Plan). Read Genesis 1-11 and the New Testament (NT) three times. Afterwards begin to read through the entire Bible chronologically.

D. **Read a Proverb and a Psalm each day** in addition to NT or OT reading.

E. **Read a single book several times in a row.** When you get to a short book like Philippians, try reading it several times in one sitting. This will help you get the big picture and better understand the details. Write down your observations. Look for themes. Construct an outline. Figure out what it means. Apply it to your life.

Don't let other studies (such as word studies, character studies, devotional guides, etc.) replace systematic reading of the Bible.

Use a System for Remembering

Have you ever read your Bible, closed it, and within fifteen minutes forgot what you read? Well, you're not alone. Using a system for remembering what you read will help you practice living a Christlike life each day.

A. **Keep a spiritual journal.** Write down the day's date, the references of the Scripture you read, and any insights God gave you. At the end of the week, review what the Lord taught you and evaluate how well you are practicing the truth.

Interpret the Bible Properly

Follow the **O.I.A.** method: **O**bservation, **I**nterpretation, **A**pplication. You must follow these steps in order if you want to correctly apply God's Word today. But don't follow them stiffly and scientifically as if you were in a chemistry lab. Remember to talk with God as you study his Word. The Bible is his love letter to you.

/ OBSERVATION /

("Just the facts, ma'am!") Before you can properly understand how the Scriptures apply to your life, you must understand what the divinely-inspired biblical author meant to communicate to the people who first received God's Word. Imagine yourself as a spiritual detective. You must first gather the facts before drawing any conclusions.

Ask: *What do I see?*

Guidelines:

- Read carefully, thoughtfully, and prayerfully.

- Ask questions. Who? What? When? Where? Why? How?

- Look for historical clues.

- Watch for key words. Key words stand out because of repetition, position, or other forms of emphasis.

- Notice things that are alike and unlike. Ideas, cultures, words, actions, commands, and many other things will have similarities or differences.

- Look for relationships between people, places, ideas, and words.

- Use resources such as a Bible dictionary, handbook, and atlas to find information on the culture, geography, and history in which the passage of Scripture originated.

- Summarize your observations by writing them in your spiritual journal.

For more help on the "observation" step, read **"The Student, the Fish, and Agassiz."**

/ INTERPRETATION /

Facts on their own don't mean much. They must be seen as part of a bigger, unifying picture. That's why interpretation comes next. This is when the detective "puts the pieces together" and comes up with an explanation of how everything happened.

Ask: *What did this mean then?*

Guidelines:

- Understand the historical context.

- Pay attention to the literary context.

    - **Give priority to paragraphs.** Words need sentences to give them meaning. And sentences need paragraphs. You, therefore, should pay careful attention to paragraphs—the basic unit of thought. Of course, paragraphs link together to paint the big picture, so read the paragraphs before and after a text you are studying in order to properly interpret it.

    - **Identify the genre and figures of speech.** Even though the Bible is one book, it contains many different types (or genres) of literature, such as poetry, narrative (or stories), letters, prophecies, and proverbs. The Bible also contains many figures of speech. Jesus, for instance, used a metaphor to talk about himself in John 6:53-58 and used hyperbole (exaggeration) in Matthew 5:29 (look up these verses). If you don't recognize literary genres and figures of speech you could end up confused and in a lot of pain!

    - **Notice grammatical details.** In Galatians 2:20 the Apostle Paul used a verb in the perfect tense: "... I have been crucified." This meant that Paul did not have to crucify himself again and again to live God's way. He already had been crucified. Instead, Paul lived every moment by faith ("live" is a present tense verb in the text).

- Understand the theological context. God has progressively revealed over a long period of time more and more about himself and his redemptive plan. When you read the OT, therefore, remember that the people to whom it was originally given did not know all the details about God's plan that we know now. The gospel is a "mystery that has been kept hidden for ages and generations, but is now disclosed to the saints." (Col 1:25-27)

- Keep asking and answering questions. If necessary, consult a commentary or ask a respected student of the Bible for their perspective on the passage.

/ APPLICATION /

Finally, we arrive to the part that transforms our lives. After all the detective work, we reach conclusions about how we should think and live. Apply God's Word to yourself first and then to your world (family, church, school, government, etc.).

Ask: *How does this apply today?*

Guidelines:

- Know the text! Remember, there is only one correct interpretation. But there are many correct applications.

- Keep Christ at the center. Always look through the lens of Christ's life, death, and resurrection when you apply Scripture. As a Christian, you are "in Christ." In him you released your sin (and its eternal consequences) and became righteous in God's sight (2 Cor 5:21). In him you can live a holy life in obedience to God's commands (2 Pet 1:3-4; Titus 2:11-14).

- Find the principle that lies beneath the meaning communicated to the original recipients. How? Look for similarities between "us" and "them"—between the original recipients and us today.

    You try it! Read 1 Corinthians 8:10-13 and find the principle that applies today. What did it mean in 57 A.D. (that is the "interpretation" step)? Answer: Don't eat what was sacrificed to idols if it will cause a former idolater to sin by eating such food against his conscience—he thinks it is wrong even though it isn't. What principle can we apply (this is the "application" step)? Don't drink alcohol in front of an alcoholic and thus encourage him to drink what causes him to fall into sin.

- Ask and answer questions. How should I respond to God? Who does the Scripture say that I am? How does the Scripture say I should live? What privilege or promise should I claim? What responsibilities do I have? What examples are given for me to follow? Is there a sin to avoid?

- Meditate. This is one of the most neglected areas of the Christian life. You must meditate on Scripture in order to gain the most from it. This involves prayerful, focused reflection on the meaning and significance of the text. You can only meditate on small portions at a time—a single paragraph, sentence, phrase, or even word.

- Make changes. Immediately put into practice what God teaches you (Jam 1:25). Make a plan of action and follow through on it. Ask God to help you obey.

Get Started!

Invest fifteen minutes of each day studying the Bible for five days per week. On Saturday or Sunday read for an hour.

Resources for Further Investigation

R. A. Torrey, *How to Study the Bible* (New Kensington, PA: Whitaker House, 1985).

Howard G. Hendricks and William D. Hendricks, *Living By the Book* (Chicago: Moody Press, 1991).

Robert H. Stein, *A Basic Guide to Interpreting the Bible* (Grand Rapids: Baker Books, 1994).

How to Study the BIBLE

WHAT: After all the detective work, we reach conclusions about how we should think and live.

ASK: How does this apply today?

Practical Tool:
1. How am I to daily live?
2. How am I daily living?
3. What changes or growth do I need to make?

APPLICATION

WHAT: This is when the detective "puts the pieces together" and comes up with an explanation of how the facts fit within the bigger picture.

ASK: What did this mean then?

Practical Tools: Commentaries, Study Bibles, Trusted Pastors and Scholars etc.

INTERPRETATION

WHAT: Imagine yourself as a spiritual detective. You must first gather the facts before drawing any conclusions.

ASK: What do I see? who, what, when, where, why & how

Practical Tools: Bible Dictionaries, Historical Texts, Ancient Maps, Hebrew / Greek Lexicons etc.

OBSERVATION

THE STUDENT, THE FISH & AGASSIZ

Take Your Bible Studies Deeper

Bible Study

Bible study consists of three important steps: **observation**, **interpretation**, and **application**. Observation is the foundation. Without good observation, you will rarely understand the right meaning or apply the Scriptures to your life properly. As you read the following story, put yourself in the student's place and think of the Bible as the fish with which the student spends so much time.

Enjoy… and ask God to stretch your powers of observation!

It was more than fifteen years ago that I entered the laboratory of Professor Agassiz and told him that I had enrolled my name in the scientific school as a student of natural history. He asked me a few questions about my object in coming, my antecedents generally, the mode in which I afterwards proposed to use the knowledge I might acquire, and finally, whether I wished to study any special branch. To the latter I replied that while I wished to be well-grounded in all departments of zoology, I purposed to devote myself specially to insects.

"When do you wish to begin?" he asked.

"Now," I replied.

This seemed to please him, and with an energetic "Very well," he took from a shelf a huge jar of specimens in yellow alcohol.

"Take this fish," said he, "and look at it; we call it a Haemulon (pronounced Hem-yulon); by and by I will ask what you have seen."

With that he left me, but in a moment returned with explicit instructions as to the care of the object entrusted to me.

"No man is fit to be a naturalist," said he, "who does not know how to take care of specimens."

I was to keep the fish before me in a tin tray, and occasionally moisten the surface with alcohol from the jar, always taking care to replace the stopper tightly. Those were not the days of ground glass stoppers and elegantly shaped exhibition jars; all the old students will recall the huge, neckless glass bottles and their leaky, wax-besmeared corks, half eaten by insects and begrimed with cellar dust. Entomology was a cleaner science than ichthyology, but the example of the professor who had unhesitatingly plunged to the bottom of the jar to produce the fish was infectious; and though this alcohol had "a very ancient and fishlike smell," I really dared not to show any aversion within these sacred precincts, and treated the alcohol as though it were pure water. Still I was conscious of a passing feeling of disappointment, for gazing at a fish did not commend itself to an ardent entomologist. My friends at home, too, were annoyed when they discovered that no amount of Eau de Cologne would drown the perfume which haunted me like a shadow.

In ten minutes I had seen all that could be seen in that fish, and started in search of the professor who had, however, left the museum; and when I returned, after lingering over some of the old animals stored in the upper apartment, I found my specimen to be dry all over. I dashed the fluid over the fish as if to resuscitate it from a fainting spell, and looked with anxiety for a return of the normal, sloppy appearance. This little excitement over, nothing was to be done but return to a steadfast gaze at my mute companion. Half an hour passed, an hour, another hour; the fish began to look loathsome. I turned it over and around, looked at it in the face—ghastly; I looked at it from behind, beneath, above, sideways, at a three-quarters' view—just as ghastly. I was in despair. At an early hour I concluded that lunch was necessary; so with infinite relief, I carefully replaced the fish in the jar, and for an hour I was free.

On my return, I learned that Professor Agassiz had been at the museum, but had gone and would not return for several hours. My fellow students were too busy to be disturbed by continued conversations. Slowly I drew forth that hideous fish, and with a feeling of desperation looked at it again. I might not use a magnifying glass; instruments of all kinds were interdicted. My two hands, my two eyes, and the fish—it seemed a most limited field. I pushed my fingers down its throat to see how sharp its teeth were. I began to count the scales in the different rows until I was convinced that that was nonsense. At last a happy thought struck me—I would draw the fish—and now with surprise I began to discover new features in the creature. Just then the professor returned.

"That is right," said he, "a pencil is one of the best eyes. I am glad to notice, too, that you keep your specimen wet and your bottle corked." With these encouraging words he added, "Well, what is it like?"

He listened attentively to my brief rehearsal to the structure of parts whose names were still unknown to me: the fringed gill—arches and movable operculum; the pores of the head, fleshy lips, and lidless eyes; the lateral line, the spinous fin, and forked tail; the compressed and arched body.

When I had finished, he waited as if expecting more, and then, with an air of disappointment, he said, "You have not looked very carefully." He continued, more earnestly, "You haven't seen one of the most conspicuous features of the animal, which is as plainly before your eyes as the fish itself. Look again! look again!" and he left me to my misery.

I was piqued; I was mortified. Still more of that wretched fish? But now I set myself to the task with a will, and discovered one new thing after another, until I saw how just the professor's criticism had been.

The afternoon passed quickly, and then, towards its close, the professor inquired, "Do you see it yet?"

"No," I replied, "I am certain I do not, but I see how little I saw before."

"That is the next best," said he earnestly, "but I won't hear you now; put away your fish an go home; perhaps you will be ready with a better answer in the morning. I will examine you then, before you look at the fish."

This was disconcerting. Not only must I think of my fish all night, studying, without the object before me, what this unknown but most visible feature might be, but also, without reviewing my new discoveries, I must give an exact account of them the next day. I had a bad memory; so I walked home by Charles River in a distracted state, with my perplexities.

The cordial greeting from the professor the next morning was reassuring. Here was a man who seemed to be quite as anxious as I that I should see for myself what he saw. "Do you perhaps mean," I asked, "that the fish has symmetrical sides with paired organs?"

His thoroughly pleased, "Of course, of course!" repaid the wakeful hours of the previous night. After he had discoursed most happily and enthusiastically, as he always did, upon the importance of this point, I ventured to ask what I should do next.

"Oh, look at your fish!" he said, and then left me again to my own devices. In a little more than an hour he returned and heard my new catalogue.

"That is good, that is good!" he repeated, "but that is not all; go on." And so, for three long days he placed that fish before my eyes, forbidding me to look at anything else, or to use any artificial aid. "Look, look, look," was his repeated injunction.

This was the best entomological lesson I ever had, and a lesson whose influence was extended to the details of every subsequent study. It was a legacy the professor has left to me, as he left it to many others, a legacy if inestimable value, which we could not but, which we cannot part.

A year afterwards, some of us were amusing ourselves with chalking outlandish beasts upon the blackboard. We drew prancing starfishes; frogs in mortal combat; hydro-headed worms; stately crawfishes standing on their tails, bearing aloft umbrellas; and grotesque fishes with gaping mouths and staring eyes. The professor came in shortly after, and was as much amused as any at our experiments. He looked at the fishes.

"Haemulons, every one of them," he said, "Mr.___ drew them."

True; and to this day, if I attempt to draw a fish, I can draw nothing but Haemulons.

The fourth day a second fish of the same group was placed beside the first, and I was bidden to point out the resemblances and the difference between the two; another and another followed, until the entire family lay before me, and a whole legion of jars covered the table and surrounding shelves. The odor had become a pleasant perfume, and even now the sight of an old, six-inch, worm-eaten cork brings fragrant memories!

The whole group of Haemulons was thus brought into view; and whether engaged upon the dissection of the bony framework, or the description of the various parts, Agassiz's training in the method of observing facts and their orderly arrangement, was ever accomplished by the urgent exhortation not to be content with them.

"Facts are stupid things," he would say, "until brought into connection with some general law."

At the end of eight months, it was almost with reluctance that I left these friends and turned to insects; but what I gained by this outside experience has been of greater value than the years of later investigation in my favorite groups.

Source: Appendix, *American Poems* [probably Boston: Houghton, Osgood and Co., 1880] *in* Irving L. Jensen, *Independent Bible Study* [Chicago: Moody Press, 1963], 141-43.

THE 8IGHT PRIORITIES

Preferred Future

Disciple-Making Pathway

8ight Priorities

Current Reality

Why it Matters: It causes us to do the most important things first so we can live an abundant life. Success is knowing what appointments to keep.

The Life Plan is an integrated whole to be lived out by faith each day until it is the lifestyle of the disciple-maker.

THE 8IGHT PRIORITIES

Success is Knowing What Appointments to Keep

A Priority List

If we put the most important things into our life first, then the many other things will fit around them. If we put the many other things into our life first, then some of the most important things will not fit. To live like Christ, we must live according to the priorities He established.

 ### Time with God

To Know God through His word and prayer.

Look it up:

God's word: Psalm 119:105; John 8:31-32; Ephesians 6:10-17; Colossians 3:16; 2 Timothy 3:16-17; Hebrews 4:12

Prayer: Mathew 6:9-13; 7:7-11; Luke 18:1; Ephesians 6:18; 1 Thessalonians 5:17; Hebrews 4:16; James 1:5; 1 John 5:14-15; John 15:7 (abide, remain, and live translate the same Greek word in John 15:7; 1 John 3:24)

 ### Time with Spouse

To make radiant, to promote health and strength, to foster love and to cherish.

Look it up: Ephesians 5:22-28; Titus 2:4-5; 1 Peter 3:1-7

 ### Time with Children

To Train in God's Word and in godliness.

Look it up: Deuteronomy 6:4-7; Proverbs 6:20; Ephesians 6:4; 1 Timothy 5:4; Titus 2:4-5

 ### Time with Parents

To learn, love and grow.

Look it up: Deuteronomy 6:4-7; Proverbs 6:20; Ephesians 6:1-3; 1 Timothy 5:4

Time at Work
To gain material provision and to witness about Christ.

> Look it up: Proverbs 14:23; Ephesians 4:28; Colossians 3:23-24; 1 Thessalonians 2:9; 2 Thessalonians 3:10; 1 Timothy 5:8

Time with Unsaved People
To witness in word and deed.

> Look it up: Proverbs 11:30; Matthew 28:19; 1 Thessalonians 1:9-10; Philippians 1:18

Time with Saved People
To build up others and to be built up.

> Look it up: 1 Corinthians 12:7; Ephesians 4:15-16; Galatians 6:1; Hebrews 10:24-25

Time at Rest
To get refreshed in order to continue doing God's work well.

> Look it up: Genesis 2:2; Exodus 23:12; Mark 6:30-31

THE 8IGHT PRIORITIES

Success is Knowing What Appointments to Keep

If we put the most important things into our life first, then the many other things will fit around them. If we put the many other things into our life first, then some of the most important things will not fit. To live like Christ, we must live according to the priorities He established.

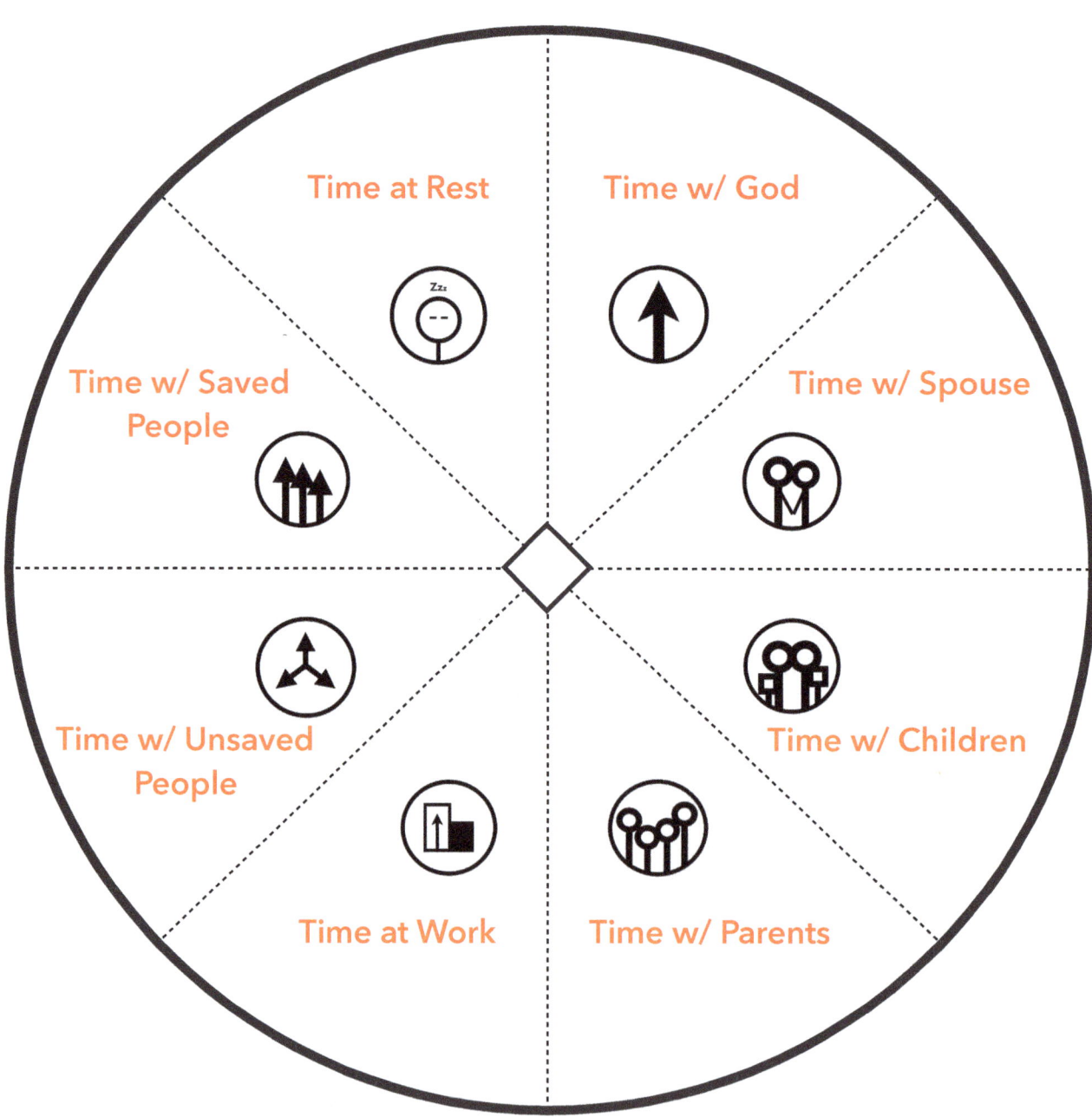

MILK OF THE WORD

Preferred Future

Disciple-Making Pathway — Milk of the Word

Current Reality

Why it Matters: It gets us on the path of righteousness and keeps us there.

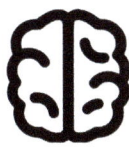

The Life Plan is an integrated whole to be lived out by faith each day until it is the lifestyle of the disciple-maker.

MILK OF THE WORD

INTRODUCTION

Hebrews 5:11-14

We have much to say about this, but it is hard to explain because you are **slow to learn.** In fact, though by this time you ought to be teachers, you need someone to teach you the **elementary truths of God's** word all over again. You need **milk**, not **solid food**! Anyone who lives on milk, being still an infant, is not acquainted with the teaching about righteousness. But **solid food** is for the mature, who by constant use have trained themselves to distinguish good from evil.

Intro

Hebrews 6:1-2 Therefore let us leave the **elementary teachings about Christ** and go on to maturity, not laying again the foundation of repentance from acts that lead to death, and of faith in God, ² instruction about baptisms, the laying on of hands, the resurrection of the dead, and eternal judgment.

1 Corinthians 3:1-3 Brothers, I could not address you as spiritual but as **worldly**-- mere infants in Christ. ² I gave you **milk**, not **solid food**, for you were not yet ready for it. Indeed, you are still not ready. ³ You are still **worldly**. For since there is jealousy and quarreling among you, are you not worldly? Are you not acting like mere men?

1 Peter 2:1-2 Therefore, rid yourselves of all malice and all deceit, hypocrisy, envy, and slander of every kind. Like newborn babies, crave pure spiritual **milk**, so that by it you may grow up in your salvation…

In the **Hebrews 5:11-14 / 6:1-2** passages above, we have two types of teaching that are essential for developing a believer in the Lord Jesus Christ:

1. **Milk of the Word:** the elementary truths of God's Word (Hebrews 5:12) or elementary teachings about Christ (Hebrew 6:1) which are foundational for the Christian. The foundational teachings are: **repentance from acts that lead to death, and of faith in God, ² instruction about baptisms, the laying on of hands, the resurrection of the dead, and eternal judgment.**

2. **Meat of the Word:** teaching about righteousness or solid food (Hebrew 5:13, 14) brings us to maturity. Teaching about righteousness is two-fold: **we are made righteous immediately upon the forgiveness of sin by belief in the gospel** (Romans 10:9-10; 1 Corinthians 15:3-4; Romans 5:1) and **we experience righteousness as we obey the Lord Jesus Christ** (Romans 6:16).

Three types of believers need the Milk of the Word:

1. **Lazy to learn** Christians. (Hebrews 5:11 - translates, "slow to learn", or "dull of hearing")

2. Believers who **live according to the flesh** or who are **worldly.** (1 Corinthians 3:1-3)

3. **New** or **infant** believers. (1 Peter 2:2)

All believers need to learn and have ready to use in an instant the foundational **Milk of the Word**. Just as we first build the foundation of a house and then build the house upon it, so we lay the foundation, **Milk of the Word**, and build upon it with teachings about righteousness, the commands of Christ (solid food). Likewise, the **Milk of the Word** keeps the mature believer on the path of righteousness, as well, it steers them back on the path when they depart from it through sin.

REPENTANCE FROM DEAD WORKS

Milk of the Word

Definition: Repent

[BDAG] μετανοέω (metanoeō)
1. change one's mind;

2. feel remorse, repent, be converted (in a variety of relationships and in connection with, varied responsibilities, moral, political, social or religious.

1. True repentance is a change of mind that produces godly actions.

Acts 26:20 First to those in Damascus, then to those in Jerusalem and in all Judea, and to the Gentiles also, **I preached that they should repent and turn to God and prove their repentance by their deeds**.

2. God commands all people everywhere to repent.

Acts 17:30-31 In the past God overlooked such ignorance, but now he commands all people everywhere to repent. ³¹ For he has set a day when he will judge the world with justice by the man he has appointed. He has given proof of this to all men by raising him from the dead.

3. God desires everyone to come to repentance.

2 Peter 3:9 The Lord is not slow in keeping his promise, as some understand slowness. He is patient with you, **not wanting anyone to perish, but everyone to come to repentance.**

4. God initiates repentance.

Luke 5:32 I have not **come to call** the righteous, but **sinners to repentance**.

Acts 11:18 When they heard this, they had no further objections and praised God, saying, "So then, **God has granted even the Gentiles repentance.**

5. People are given opportunity to repent.

Romans 2:4 Or do you show contempt for the riches of his kindness, tolerance and patience, not realizing that **God's kindness leads you toward repentance?**

Romans 5:8 But God demonstrates his own love for us in this: While we were still sinners, Christ died for us. (greatest act of kindness)

2 Corinthians 7:8-10 Even if I caused you sorrow by my letter, I do not regret it. Though I did regret it-- I see that my letter hurt you, but only for a little while-- ⁹ yet now I am happy, not because you were made sorry, but because **your sorrow led you to repentance.** For you became sorrowful as God intended and so were not harmed in any way by us. ¹⁰ **Godly sorrow brings repentance that leads to salvation** and leaves no regret, but worldly sorrow brings death.

2 Timothy 2:25 Those who oppose him he **must gently instruct, in the hope that God will grant them repentance** leading them to a knowledge of the truth,

6. We can hear God considers something sin and not repent.

John 3:19-20 This is the verdict: Light has come into the world, but men loved darkness instead of light because their deeds were evil. ²⁰ Everyone who does evil hates the light, and will not come into the light for fear that his deeds will be exposed.

2 Corinthians 7:8-10 Even if I caused you sorrow by my letter, I do not regret it. Though I did regret it-- I see that my letter hurt you, but only for a little while-- ⁹ yet now I am happy, not because you were made sorry, but because your sorrow led you to repentance. For you became sorrowful as God intended and so were not harmed in any way by us. ¹⁰ Godly sorrow brings repentance that leads to salvation and leaves no regret, but **worldly sorrow brings death.**

7. Repentance leads to release from the penalty of sin. (Unbeliever)

Illustration: Clean slate, concerning the penalty of sin.

Mark 1:15 "The time has come," he said. "The kingdom of God is near. Repent and believe the good news!"

8. Repentance leads to restored fellowship with God. (Believer)

Illustration: Slate kept clean, concerning fellowship with God.

1 John 1:9 If we confess our sins, he is faithful and just and will forgive us our sins and purify us from all unrighteousness.

Revelation 2:5 Remember the height from which you have fallen! **Repent and do the things you did at first.** If you do not repent, I will come to you and remove your lamp stand from its place.

 # FAITH IN GOD

Milk of the Word

Definition: Faith

[BDAG] πίστις (pistis)

1. that which evokes trust and faith

2. state of believing on the basis of the reliability of the one trusted, trust, confidence, faith in the active sense = 'believing', in ref. to deity

3. that which is believed, body of faith/belief/teaching

1. Faith to be saved from the penalty of sin

Ephesians 2:8-9 For it is **by grace you have been saved, through faith** and this not from yourselves, it is the gift of God ⁹ not by works, so that no one can boast.

Romans 5:1-2 Therefore, since **we have been justified through faith**, we {1 Or let us} have peace with God through our Lord Jesus Christ, ² through whom we have gained access by faith into this grace in which we now stand. And we {2 Or let us} rejoice in the hope of the glory of God.

2. Faith for healing.

Matthew 9:2 Some men brought to him a paralytic, lying on a mat. **When Jesus saw their faith, he said to the paralytic, "Take heart, son; your sins are forgiven."**

Matthew 9:22 Jesus turned and saw her. "Take heart, daughter," he said, **"your faith has healed you." And the woman was healed from that moment.**

Matthew 9:29 Then he touched their eyes and said, **"According to your faith will it be done to you."**

3. Faith is based not on men's wisdom, but on God's power.

1 Corinthians 2:5 so that your **faith** might not **rest** on men's wisdom, but on **God's power**.

John 2:18-22 The Jews then responded to him, "What sign can you show us to prove your authority to do all this?" ¹⁹ Jesus answered them, "Destroy this temple, and I will raise it again in three days." ²⁰ They replied, "It has taken forty-six years to build this temple, and you are going to raise it in three days?" ²¹ But the temple he had spoken of was his body. ²² After he was raised from the dead, his disciples recalled what he had said. **Then they believed the scripture and the words that Jesus had spoken.**

4. Faith is attempting to do God's will fully expecting Him to fulfill our attempt with His power.

2 Thessalonians 1:11 With this in mind, we constantly pray for you, that our God may count you worthy of his calling, and that **by his power he may fulfill every good purpose of yours and every act prompted by your faith.** (Sanctification by faith)

5. Faith accesses God's resources.

Mark 11:22-23 "Have faith in God," Jesus answered. ²³ "I tell you the truth, if anyone says to this mountain, 'Go, throw yourself into the sea,' and does not doubt in his heart **but believes that what he says will happen, it will be done for him…"**

Galatians 2:20 I have been crucified with Christ and I no longer live, but Christ lives in me. The life I live in the body, **I live by faith in the Son of God**, who loved me and gave himself for me.

6. Fear is indicative of no or little faith.

Luke 8:24-25 The disciples went and woke him, saying, "Master, Master, we're going to drown!" He got up and rebuked the wind and the raging waters; the storm subsided, and all was calm. ²⁵ "Where is your faith?" he asked his disciples. In fear and amazement they asked one another, "Who is this? He commands even the winds and the water, and they obey him."

7. Faith is how we overcome fear.

John 14:1 "Do not let your hearts be troubled. You believe in God; believe also in me."

Final Thoughts

This calls for patient endurance and faithfulness on the part of the saints.

We survive and thrive in persecution by faith in God.

Additional teaching on faith:

- Basis of faith - 1 Corinthians 15:14, 17
- How we grow in faith - Romans 10:17; 2 Thessalonians 1:3
- Faith expresses itself through love - Galatians 5:6
- Faith without works is not saving faith - James 2:14, 17, 26
- Faith is how we gain victory over the world - 1 John 5:4

2 Corinthians 12:9 But he said to me, "My grace is sufficient for you, for my power is made perfect in weakness." Therefore I will boast all the more gladly of my weaknesses, so that the power of Christ may rest upon me. ESV

Galatians 2:20 I have been crucified with Christ. It is no longer I who live, but Christ who lives in me. And the life I now live in the flesh I live by faith in the Son of God, who loved me and gave himself for me. ESV

Revelation 13:10 If anyone is to be taken captive, to captivity he goes; if anyone is to be slain with the sword, with the sword must he be slain. Here is a call for the endurance and faith of the saints. ESV

 # BAPTISMS

Milk of the Word

The Three Baptisms

John's Baptism

Baptism with the Holy Spirit

Believer's Baptism

John's Baptism (Preparatory)

Purpose: To prepare a person for salvation.

Luke 7:29-30 All the people, even the tax collectors, when they heard Jesus' words, acknowledged that God's way was right, because they had been baptized by John. ³⁰ But the Pharisees and experts in the law rejected God's purpose for themselves, because they had not been baptized by John.

Meaning: John's baptism is twofold:

1. We publicly repent of our sin. (Mark 1:4)

2. We confess our sins and acknowledge our need of forgiveness (Mark 1:5).

Mode: To dip the person under water (baptism means to dip under as seen in John baptizing Jesus recorded in Matthew 3:16).

The testimony of the Holy Spirit and the saints has replaced the practice of John's baptism (see John 15:26-27 and John 16:8-11).

Application:

- We need to remember how important the "John the Baptist" ministry was in our life. It made us aware of sin. (Rom 7:7, 13)

- We need to do our part in the "John the Baptist" ministry to prepare others to receive Jesus as their savior, that is, help people see their sin. (Rom 7:7, 13)

Baptism with the Holy Spirit (Salvatory)

Purpose: The baptism with the Holy Spirit is to resource us with everything we need to be like Christ and to do His works.

The resources we gain when we receive the gift of the Holy Spirit are as follows:

1. Guaranteed salvation. (Ephesians 1:13-14)

2. The power to be and do God's will. (Ephesians 1:19-20; Acts 1:8)

3. Guidance into all truth. (John 16:13)

4. God's promptings to specific service. (Acts 8:29)

5. We become an important part of the Body of Christ and have access to all the gifts of other parts of the Body. (1 Corinthians 12:13)

Application:

- We are to remember the resources we have received by being baptized with the Holy Spirit are sufficient for being and doing all that Jesus commands.

- We can live secure knowing we have eternal life.

- We can trust God to guide us into all truth.

- We can act in faith expecting God to fulfill our act of faith with His power. (2 Thessalonians 1:11)

- We can heed the promptings of the Holy Spirit to specific acts of service.

- We are to remember we are a significant part of the Body of Christ and need each part to accomplish the works Christ has assigned us. (1 Corinthians 11:1; Ephesians 2:10)

Believer's Baptism (Revelatory)

Purpose: Public revelation of the inner salvation by faith in Christ.

1 Peter 3:21 "Baptism, which corresponds to this, now saves you (not as the removal of dirt from the body, but the **pledge** [pledge, answer, appeal: **eperotoma**, ἐπερώτημα] of a good conscience toward God) through the resurrection of Jesus, Christ…" CSB

Meaning: The believer's baptism is our public commitment to the terms of our service for Jesus Christ. In 1 Peter 3:21 The Greek word *eperotoma* means the following: "In every business contract there was a definite question and answer which made the contract binding. The question was, 'Do you accept the terms of this contract and bind yourself to observe them?' The technical word for that question and answer clause is *eperotoma* in Greek and *stipulation* in Latin. In baptism God said to the man coming out of heathenism: 'Do you accept the terms of My service? Do you accept the privileges and promises, and do you undertake its responsibilities and demands?' And in the act of being baptized the man answered, 'Yes'." - William Barclay in the *Letters of James and Peter*.

Terms of service we agree to when we are baptized:

1. **Privileges** we have as believers:
   - Fruit of the Spirit. (Galatians 5:22-23)
   - We are chosen by Jesus to bear much fruit that remains and to have answered prayer. (John 15:16)
   - We have God's mercy and help in our time of need. (Hebrews 4:16)

2. **Promises** we have as believers:
   - We have eternal life. (John 3:16)
   - We have power to do all He commands us to do. (Ephesians 1:19-20; 3:20; Acts 1:8)
   - We have His provision. (Matthew 6:33)

3. **Responsibilities** we have as believers:
   - We are to witness to others concerning salvation in Christ. (Acts 1:8)
   - We are to go and make disciples of all nations, baptizing them in the name of the Father, and the Son, and the Holy Spirit and teach them to obey everything Jesus commanded. (Matthew 28:19-20)

4. **Demands** we have as believers:
   - We are to deny ourselves and take up our cross daily and follow Jesus. (Matthew 16:24)
   - We are to be willing to lose our life for Jesus sake. (Matthew 16:25)
   - We are to put Jesus first in all our relationships. (Luke 14:26)
   - We are to be willing to give up all we have to be Jesus' disciple. (Luke 14:33)

Remembering the Baptisms will move us to:

- Testify along with the Holy Spirit to convict people of sin, righteousness and judgment and of their need for Christ's salvation.

- Remember the terms of our service for Christ and enjoy the privileges, claim the promises, fulfill the responsibilities, and meet the demands.

- Remember the resources we have been given by Christ and use them to complete the assignments God has given each of us.

Mode of Baptism: The mode of believer's baptism is to be dipped under water as the Ethiopian eunuch was in Acts 8:38-39, "And he commanded the chariot to stop, and they both went down into the water, Philip and the eunuch, and he baptized him. [39] **And when they came up out of the water**, the Spirit of the Lord carried Philip away, and the eunuch saw him no more, and went on his way rejoicing."

Application:

- We need to remember the terms of service and fulfill them.

- We need to participate in the privileges, promises, responsibilities and demands we agreed to.

LAYING ON OF HANDS

Milk of the Word

Intro:

This doctrine is placed by the Holy Spirit as a foundation of faith, as milk for young believers. This is not a commonly practiced teaching in the church today because it is hard to understand. Since the Bible declares this as milk of the Word, we need to drink freely and practice this doctrine in our churches and families.

1. Laying on of hands to recognize or initiate into special service.

Acts 6:6 They presented these men to the apostles, who prayed and **laid their hands on them.**

Acts 13:1-3 In the church at Antioch there were prophets and teachers: Barnabas, Simeon called Niger, Lucius of Cyrene, Manaen (who had been brought up with Herod the tetrarch) and Saul. ² While they were worshiping the Lord and fasting, the Holy Spirit said, "Set apart for me Barnabas and Saul for the work to which I have called them." ³ So after they had fasted and prayed, **they placed their hands on them** and sent them off.

1 Timothy 5:22 Do not be hasty in **the laying on of hands**, and do not share in the sins of others. Keep yourself pure.

2. Laying on of hands to bless children.

Matthew 19:13-15 Then little children were **brought to Jesus for him to place his hands on them and pray for them**. But the disciples rebuked those who brought them. ¹⁴ Jesus said, "Let the little children come to me, and do not hinder them, for the kingdom of heaven belongs to such as these." ¹⁵ When **he had placed his hands on them**, he went on from there.

Mark 10:13-16 People were bringing little children to Jesus to have him touch them, but the disciples rebuked them. ¹⁴ When Jesus saw this, he was indignant. He said to them, "Let the little children come to me, and do not hinder them, for the kingdom of God belongs to such as these. ¹⁵ I tell you the truth, anyone who will not receive the kingdom of God like a little child will never enter it." ¹⁶ **And he took the children in his arms, put his hands on them and blessed them.**

3. **Laying on of hands** to gift for ministry.

    1 Timothy 4:14 Do not neglect your **gift**, which was **given** you through a prophetic message **when the body of elders laid their hands on you.**

    2 Timothy 1:6 For this reason I remind you to fan into flame **the gift of God, which is in you through the laying on of my hands.**

4. **Laying on of hands** as a way to heal.

    Mark 1:41-42 Filled with compassion, **Jesus reached out his hand and touched the man**. "I am willing**,**" he said. "Be clean!" ⁴² **Immediately the leprosy left him** and he was cured.

    Mark 6:5 He could not do any miracles there, except **lay his hands on a few sick people and heal them.**

    Acts 9:12 In a vision he has seen a man named Ananias come and **place his hands on him to restore his sight.**

    Acts 9:17-18 Then Ananias went to the house and entered it**. Placing his hands on Saul, he said,** "Brother Saul, the Lord-- Jesus, who appeared to you on the road as you were coming here-- has sent me so that you may see again and be filled with the Holy Spirit." ¹⁸ Immediately, something like scales fell from Saul's eyes, and he could see again. He got up and was baptized,

    Acts 28:8 His father was sick in bed, suffering from fever and dysentery. Paul went in to see him and**, after prayer, placed his hands on him and healed him**.

RESURRECTION OF THE DEAD

Milk of the Word

Intro:

Luke, the author of the Book of Acts, noted that Jesus, *"After his suffering, he showed himself to these men (Apostles) and gave many convincing proofs that he was alive (resurrected)."* **Acts 1:3**

To this day, the doctrine of the Resurrection is a key source of the Christian's belief, hope and obedience in Christ.

1. Documented eyewitness accounts of Jesus Christ's resurrection from the dead.

1 Corinthians 15:3-8 For what I received I passed on to you as of first importance: {3 Or you at the first} that Christ died for our sins according to the Scriptures, 4 that he was buried, that he was **raised** on the third day according to the Scriptures, 5 and that he appeared to Peter, {5 Greek Cephas} and then to the Twelve. 6 After that, he appeared to more than five hundred of the brothers at the same time, most of whom are still living, though some have fallen asleep. 7 Then he appeared to James, then to all the apostles, 8 and last of all he appeared to me also, as to one abnormally born.

1 John 1:1-3 That which was from the beginning, which we have heard, which we have seen with our eyes, which we have looked at and our hands have touched-- this we proclaim concerning the Word of life. 2 The life appeared; we have seen it and testify to it, and we proclaim to you the eternal life, which was with the Father and has appeared to us. 3 We proclaim to you what we have seen and heard, so that you also may have fellowship with us. And our fellowship is with the Father and with his Son, Jesus Christ.

2. The Basis of our Belief: Jesus Christ's resurrection from the dead.

Luke 9:22 And he said, "The Son of Man must suffer many things and be rejected by the elders, chief priests and teachers of the law, and he must be killed and on the third day be raised to life."

Luke 24:6-7 He is not here; he has risen! Remember how he told you, while he was still with you in Galilee: 7 "The Son of Man must be delivered into the hands of sinful men, be crucified and on the third day be raised again."

John 2:18-22 Then the Jews demanded of him, "What miraculous sign can you show us to prove your authority to do all this?" 19 Jesus answered them, "Destroy this temple, and I will raise it again in three days." 20 The Jews replied, "It has taken forty-six years to build this temple, and you are going to raise it in three days?" 21 But the temple he had spoken of was his body. 22 After he was raised from the dead, his disciples recalled what he had said. Then they believed the Scripture and the words that Jesus had spoken.

Acts 2:31-32 Seeing what was ahead, he spoke of the resurrection of the Christ, {*31* Or Messiah. "The Christ" (Greek) and "the Messiah" (Hebrew) both mean "the Anointed One"; also in verse 36.} that he was not abandoned to the grave, nor did his body see decay. ³² God has raised this Jesus to life, and we are all witnesses of the fact.

Acts 4:33 With great power the apostles continued to testify to the resurrection of the Lord Jesus, and much grace was upon them all."

Romans 1:3-4 regarding his Son, who as to his human nature was a descendant of David, ⁴ and who through the Spirit {*4* Or who as to his spirit} of holiness was declared with power to be the Son of God by his resurrection from the dead: Jesus Christ our Lord.

3. The Basis of our Hope: Jesus Christ's resurrection from the dead.

John 11:25-26 Jesus said to her, "I am the resurrection and the life. He who believes in me will live, even though he dies; ²⁶ and whoever lives and believes in me will never die. Do you believe this?"

Acts 4:2 They were greatly disturbed because the apostles were teaching the people and proclaiming in Jesus the resurrection of the dead.

Acts 23:6 Then Paul, knowing that some of them were Sadducees and the others Pharisees, called out in the Sanhedrin, "My brothers, I am a Pharisee, the son of a Pharisee. I stand on trial because of my hope in the resurrection of the dead."

Philippians 3:10-11 I want to know Christ and the power of his resurrection and the fellowship of sharing in his sufferings, becoming like him in his death, ¹¹ and so, somehow, to attain to the resurrection from the dead.

Romans 4:25 He was delivered over to death for our sins and was raised to life for our justification.

1 Corinthians 15:12-22 But if it is preached that Christ has been raised from the dead, how can some of you say that there is no resurrection of the dead? 13 If there is no resurrection of the dead, then not even Christ has been raised. 14 And if Christ has not been raised, our preaching is useless and so is your faith. 15 More than that, we are then found to be false witnesses about God, for we have testified about God that he raised Christ from the dead. But he did not raise him if in fact the dead are not raised. 16 For if the dead are not raised, then Christ has not been raised either. 17 And if Christ has not been raised, your faith is futile; you are still in your sins. 18 Then those also who have fallen asleep in Christ are lost. 19 If only for this life we have hope in Christ, we are to be pitied more than all men. 20 But Christ has indeed been raised from the dead, the first fruits of those who have fallen asleep. 21 For since death came through a man, the resurrection of the dead comes also through a man. 22 For as in Adam all die, so in Christ all will be made alive.

1 Peter 1:3 Praise be to the God and Father of our Lord Jesus Christ! In his great mercy he has given us new birth into a living hope through the resurrection of Jesus Christ from the dead,

4. The Basis of our Obedience Unto Death: Jesus Christ's resurrection from the dead.

1 Corinthians 15:10-11 But by the grace of God I am what I am, and his grace to me was not without effect. No, I worked harder than all of them - yet not I, but the grace of God that was with me. 11 Whether, then, it was I or they, this is what we preach, and this is what you believed.

1 Corinthians 15:19-20 If only for this life we have hope in Christ, we are to be pitied more than all men. 20 But Christ has indeed been raised from the dead, the first fruits of those who have fallen asleep.

Hebrews 11:25 He chose to be mistreated along with the people of God rather than to enjoy the pleasures of sin for a short time.

Hebrews 11:35 Women received back their dead, raised to life again. Others were tortured and refused to be released, so that they might gain a better resurrection.

Luke 14:14 and you will be blessed. Although they cannot repay you, you will be repaid at the resurrection of the righteous. **(We gain our sure reward at the resurrection.)**

5. There are two resurrections.

John 5:24-29 I tell you the truth, whoever hears my word and believes him who sent me has eternal life and will not be condemned; he has crossed over from death to life. 25 I tell you the truth, a time is coming and has now come when the dead will hear the voice of the Son of God and those who hear will live. 26 For as the Father has life in himself, so he has granted the Son to have life in himself. 27 And he has given him authority to judge because he is the Son of Man. 28 Do not be amazed at this, for a time is coming when all who are in their graves will hear his voice 29 and come out-- those who have done good will rise to live, and those who have done evil will rise to be condemned.

Acts 24:15 and I have the same hope in God as these men, that there will be a resurrection of both the righteous and the wicked.

Revelation 20:5-6 (The rest of the dead did not come to life until the thousand years were ended.) This is the first resurrection. 6 Blessed and holy are those who have part in the first resurrection. The second death has no power over them, but they will be priests of God and of Christ and will reign with him for a thousand years.

   1. **The Resurrection of the Righteous: 2 Corinthians 5:10** For we must all appear before the judgment seat of Christ, that each one may receive what is due him for the things done while in the body, whether good or bad. **(The resurrection to life.)**

   2. **The Resurrection of the Wicked: Revelation 20:11-15** Then I saw a great white throne and him who was seated on it. Earth and sky fled from his presence, and there was no place for them. 12 And I saw the dead, great and small, standing before the throne, and books were opened. Another book was opened, which is the book of life. The dead were judged according to what they had done as recorded in the books. 13 The sea gave up the dead that were in it, and death and Hades gave up the dead that were in them, and each person was judged according to what he had done. 14 Then death and Hades were thrown into the lake of fire. The lake of fire is the second death. 15 If anyone's name was not found written in the book of life, he was thrown into the lake of fire. **(Resurrection to 2nd Death.)**

6. There is no marriage after the resurrection.

Luke 20:35-36 But those who are considered worthy of taking part in that age and in the resurrection from the dead will neither marry nor be given in marriage, 36 and they can no longer die; for they are like the angels. They are God's children, since they are children of the resurrection.

7. **The Resurrection of Jesus Christ** is to be preached to the ordinary and intellectual.

Acts 17:18 A group of Epicurean and Stoic philosophers began to dispute with him. Some of them asked, "What is this babbler trying to say?" Others remarked, "He seems to be advocating foreign gods." They said this because Paul was preaching the good news about Jesus and the resurrection. **(Preached to intellectuals.)**

1 Corinthians 1:26 Brothers, think of what you were when you were called. Not many of you were wise by human standards; not many were influential; not many were of noble birth." **(Preached to ordinary with accepting response.)**

Acts 17:32 When they heard about the resurrection of the dead, some of them sneered, but others said, "We want to hear you again on this subject." **(The response of the intellectual.)**

ETERNAL JUDGEMENT

Milk of the Word

Eternal Punishment

Matthew 25:46 Then they will go away to **eternal** punishment, but the righteous to **eternal** life.

GNT **Matthew 25:46** καὶ ἀπελεύσονται οὗτοι εἰς κόλασιν **αἰώνιον** οἱ δὲ δίκαιοι εἰς ζωὴν **αἰώνιον**

In Matthew 25:46, the author makes clear that Jesus teaches there is an eternal punishment, as sure as there is an eternal life. The word eternal is highlighted in bold print in both the English and the Greek text. Although you may not read Greek, you can see the word is the same when used to modify both punishment and life.

Romans 3:21-26 But now a righteousness from God, apart from law, has been made known, to which the Law and the Prophets testify. 22 This righteousness from God comes through faith in Jesus Christ to all who believe. There is no difference, 23 for all have sinned and fall short of the glory of God, 24 and are justified freely by his grace through the redemption that came by Christ Jesus. 25 God presented him as a sacrifice of atonement, {25 or as the one who would turn aside his wrath, taking away sin} through faith in his blood. He did this to demonstrate his justice, because in his forbearance he had left the sins committed beforehand unpunished - 26 he did it to demonstrate his justice at the present time, so as to be just and the one who justifies those who have faith in Jesus.

These verses (Matthew 25:46 & Romans 3:21-26) show us that we are made righteous by faith in Jesus Christ's death on the cross.

NKJ **John 3:36** He who believes in the Son has everlasting life; and he who does not believe the Son shall not see life, but the wrath of God abides on him.

Jude 1:7 In a similar way, Sodom and Gomorrah and the surrounding towns gave themselves up to sexual immorality and perversion. They serve as an example of those who suffer the punishment of eternal fire.

Revelation 21:8 But the cowardly, the unbelieving, the vile, the murderers, the sexually immoral, those who practice magic arts, the idolaters and all liars-- their place will be in the fiery lake of burning sulfur. This is the second death.

Acts 10:42 He **commanded** us to preach to the people and to testify that he is the one whom God appointed as judge of the living and the dead.

Acts 17:30-31 In the past God overlooked such ignorance, but now he **commands** all people everywhere to repent. ³¹ For he has set a day when he will judge the world with justice by the man he has appointed. He has given proof of this to all men by raising him from the dead.

1. The Judgment of the Person Who Did Not Repent and Believe the Gospel.

Revelation 20:11-15 Then I saw a great white throne and him who was seated on it. Earth and sky fled from his presence, and there was no place for them. ¹² And I saw the dead, great and small, standing before the throne, and books were opened. Another book was opened, which is the book of life. The dead were judged according to what they had done as recorded in the books. ¹³ The sea gave up the dead that were in it, and death and Hades gave up the dead that were in them, and each person was judged according to what he had done. ¹⁴ Then death and Hades were thrown into the lake of fire. The lake of fire is the second death. ¹⁵ If anyone's name was not found written in the book of life, he was thrown into the lake of fire.

Note: In verse 15 the grammar reveals that no one appearing before the Great White Throne had his name written in the book of life. All appearing were unbelievers. Believers will appear before Jesus to be judged for a final time also. At that judgment each will receive a reward for the good that has been recorded in the book of their life and pardon for the sin recorded in that same book. See 1 Corinthians 3:10-15; 2 Corinthians 5:10. The pardon for sin is received because each believer's name is recorded in the Lamb's book of life because they believed in Jesus.

Below, **Luke 16:19-31** reveals the picture of eternal torment.

Luke 16:19-31 There was a rich man who was dressed in purple and fine linen and lived in luxury every day. ²⁰ At his gate was laid a beggar named Lazarus, covered with sores ²¹ and longing to eat what fell from the rich man's table. Even the dogs came and licked his sores. ²² The time came when the beggar died and the angels carried him to Abraham's side. The rich man also died and was buried. ²³ In hell, {23 Greek Hades} where he was in torment, he looked up and saw Abraham far away, with Lazarus by his side. ²⁴ So he called to him, "Father Abraham, have pity on me and send Lazarus to dip the tip of his finger in water and cool my tongue, because I am in **agony in this fire**." ²⁵ But Abraham replied, "Son, remember that in your lifetime you received your good things, while Lazarus received bad things, but now he is comforted here and you are in agony. **²⁶ And besides all this, between us and you a great chasm has been fixed, so that those who want to go from here to you cannot, nor can anyone cross over from there to us."** ²⁷ "He answered, "Then I beg you, father, send Lazarus to my father's house, ²⁸ for I have five brothers. Let him warn them, so that they will not also come to **this place of torment."** ²⁹ "Abraham replied, "They have Moses and the Prophets; let them listen to them." ³⁰ "No, father Abraham," he said, "but if someone from the dead goes to them, they will repent." ³¹ He said to him, "If they do not listen to Moses and the Prophets, they will not be convinced even if someone rises from the dead."

2. The Judgment of the Person Who Repented and Believed the Gospel.

2 Corinthians 5:10 For we must all appear before the judgment seat of Christ, so that each of us may receive what is due us for the things done while in the body, whether good or bad.

1 Corinthians 3:1-3, 10-15 Brothers and sisters, I could not address you as **people who live by the Spirit** but as **people who are still worldly - mere infants in Christ.** ² I gave you milk, not solid food, for you were not yet ready for it. Indeed, you are still not ready. ³ You are still worldly. For since there is jealousy and quarreling among you, are you not worldly? Are you not acting like mere humans? …¹⁰ By the grace God has given me, I laid a foundation as a wise builder, and someone else is building on it. But each one should build with care. ¹¹ For no one can lay any foundation other than the one already laid, which is Jesus Christ. ¹² If anyone builds on this foundation using gold, silver, costly stones, wood, hay or straw, ¹³ their work will be shown for what it is, because the Day will bring it to light. It will be revealed with fire, and the fire will test the quality of each person's work. ¹⁴ **If what has been built survives, the builder will receive a reward.** ¹⁵ **If it is burned up, the builder will suffer loss but yet will be saved - even though only as one escaping through the flames.**

Why is eternal judgement foundational?

Knowledge of eternal judgment gives the believer motivation to forsake sinful ways and imitate Jesus and to seek to get the message of salvation to those who haven't repented and believed the gospel.

Proverbs 27:12 The prudent see danger and take refuge, but the simple keep going and suffer for it.

Proverbs 10:29 The way of the Lord is a refuge for the righteous, but it is the ruin of those who do evil.

Note: 1 Corinthians 3:1 tells us of two types of Christians, the Christian living according to God's will and the Christian who is living according to the ways of the world (sin nature). The believer in Jesus Christ will be judged for his works. The works of sin will be burned up and the person will be pardoned and saved (1 Corinthians 3:15) and will be rewarded for the works done according to God's will (1 Corinthians 3:14).

MEAT OF THE WORD

Preferred Future

Discipline-Making Pathway

Meat of the Word

Current Reality

Why it Matters: It grows us to maturity in Christ.

The Life Plan is an integrated whole to be lived out by faith each day until it is the lifestyle of the disciple-maker.

MEAT OF THE WORD

Grace to Obey

The Apostle Paul wrote to the Corinthian church, "The only thing that counts is obeying His commands" (1 Cor 7:19). Trust and obey for there's no other way to be happy in Jesus but to trust and obey.

Salvation comes entirely by the grace of God. It is important to note, however, that just as we are righteous in Christ by grace through faith (Ephesians 2:8-9; Romans 5:1-2; Hebrews 10:14), so in the same way do we live out our righteousness: by grace through faith (2 Corinthians 12:9; Hebrews 4:16; 10:14; Galatians 2:20). Eternal life and abundant life are both experienced by grace through faith.

Intro

Abundant life. That's what everyone's looking for, isn't it? Life to the fullest? Good news: Jesus offers that kind of life. He came that we might have life and have it abundantly (John 10:10b). Disciples are introduced to the foundations of an abundant Christian life in the Milk of the Word. Yet the author of Hebrews encourages that it's the teaching on righteousness, or solid food (Heb. 5:13-14), that brings us to maturity.

Jesus stated in nine words the curriculum for abundant living, "teaching them to obey everything I have commanded you" (Matthew 28:20). The Milk of the Word is vital to knowing and growing in Christ. The Meat of the Word carries us onward in a Spirit-filled, obedient righteousness that will make a positive difference in raising children, having a fulfilling godly marriage, in doing business, within our friendships and in everything we are and do no matter the circumstances. Obedience to His commands displays God's glory to a lost and dying world.

Disciple-makers are not only nourished on the Milk of the Word, but daily practice the Meat of the Word and experience the blessings of Christlike maturity.

Our Confidence to Obey: Knowing God

We have confidence to obey the Lord because His purpose is for us to have eternal and abundant life. These purposes are clearly stated in John 3:16 and John 10:10b: "For God so loved the world that he gave his one and only Son, that whoever believes in him shall not perish but have eternal life" and "The thief comes only to steal and kill and destroy; I came that they may have life, and have it abundantly" (emphasis added). The Lord desires for us to be with Him forever (John 14:1-6) and that we experience fullness of life here on earth, even within an environment corrupted by sin (Romans 3:23; 5:12; 8:21,22; Philippians 2:15).

We have confidence to obey the Lord because, as Creator, He knows what is best for us. He knows how we are made (Psalm 139:13-16, Genesis 1:27). He knows what we need (Matthew 6:8,31,32). The Lord, as Creator, has all the power needed to do whatever He commands (Genesis 1:3, 6, 9, 11, etc.).

We have confidence to obey the Lord because His actions have given us reason to believe he has our best interests in mind. The Lord's desire for our best interests is made crystal clear by Romans 5:8 and

Romans 8:31-32. The Lord made the greatest sacrifice anyone could make to demonstrate His love for us. He clarified in 8:31 that He is for us and in 8:32 that He will spare nothing for our well-being. We can confidently and eagerly obey Him!

We need confidence in the Lord in order to obey him. For instance, the commands to rejoice, be glad and leap for joy seem rather odd to be following when we are insulted, persecuted, and falsely accused because of Jesus. But that is exactly what Jesus commands believers to do in Matthew 5:11-12 and Luke 6:23. We can trust and obey because we know the Lord.

The Need to Obey: We are Blind

The Lord makes it very clear through the written Word that people are blind, and they don't know they're blind unless it is revealed to them by the Holy Spirit using the written Word (John 16:8-11; Romans 7:7,13). Proverbs 14:12 and 4:19 state this truth: people do what they think is right for them at the time they do it and don't really know why they stumbled and messed up their life (they did what they thought was right). Some go through life without living God's way and are not aware of the destruction until it suddenly comes upon them at the end of their lives (Psalm 73:4, 5, 18-20).

We are blind because of sin's deception. Sin deceives us and hardens our heart to the truth (Hebrews 3:12-13). We are determined to do what we think is right and best for us, but because sin is pleasurable for a season of time (Hebrews 11:25), we are deceived and stumble in the darkness of that deception. We are blind and don't know it – unless we take the Scripture as truth. If we believe that the Scripture is true, then we realize we are blind and in darkness and we seek light and assistance in living life so we can avoid stumbling and ruining ourselves.

We are blind as people because the god of this age has blinded the minds of unbelievers (2 Corinthians 4:4). If we are unbelievers we are blinded to the truth and walk in darkness (Ephesians 2:1-3; 4:17-19). We can walk in darkness as believers if we continue to live like unbelievers in the futility of our own thinking (Ephesians 4:17) and don't continually renew our mind in the truth and put it into practice (Ephesians 4:20-24; Romans 12:2). Satan, the god of this age, deceives even believers if the believers do not stand firm in the truth (1 Peter 5:8-9; 2 Corinthians 11:3).

Psalm 19:8 and Proverbs 6:23 state clearly that God's commands give light in darkness. Jesus commanded that His new disciples be taught to obey everything He commanded the disciples who had followed Him during His three years of teaching (Matthew 28:20). We need to learn and obey the commands of God if we are to experience eternal and abundant life. We will not be deceived if we obey the commands of the Lord Jesus Christ, the Creator God.

The Psalmist called God's commands a lamp (Psalm 19:8). If we realize we are in darkness, then we desire to have the lamp of His commands. We are commanded, for instance, in Matthew 5:24 to make it a priority, even over offering sacrifice to the Lord, to be reconciled with people. This works to light up our relationships. If we don't realize we are in darkness and think we are in the light (i.e., that we're right), then we are in the dark in many relationships and miss out on the blessing the Lord desires for us.

The Power to Obey: We Can Obey

We, who are powerless on our own to consistently obey His commands, can obey all His commands consistently by using His power. He gives us the grace to obey (1 Peter 5:10; Titus 2:11-14). As believers in Christ we can no longer say, "I can't obey." Instead, when we are failing to obey His commands, we more truthfully must say, "I won't obey."

An example of a command that seems too difficult to obey is found in Luke 17:3-4. In those verses, we are commanded to rebuke the one who sins against us and forgive him if he repents. We are commanded to forgive even seven times in one day. Even though it seems very difficult to obey that command, we have the power to do it.

We, as believers in Jesus Christ have the power to obey everything we are commanded to do by our Lord Jesus Christ. God promised to give us His Spirit to enable us to obey (see Ezekiel 36:27). We received His promised Holy Spirit when we believed the truth of the gospel (Ephesians 1:13-14). The Holy Spirit is God dwelling in us. He empowers us to be able to obey the truth continuously. We can do beyond what we can think or imagine according to His power at work within us (Ephesians 3:20). We can do all things He commands us to do because He is in us strengthening us (Philippians 4:13).

We exercise the power we have by continuously exercising faith as Paul states in Galatians 2:20. Living by faith can be defined as follows: "attempting to obey expecting the Lord to fulfill our act of faith with His power" (see Paul's prayer in 2 Thessalonians 1:11). We can obey every command the Lord has given us. The command may seem impossible for us to do, but if we attempt to obey, the Lord will do for us and through us what is impossible for us to do without Him (NOTE: John 15:5 states very clearly that apart from Him we can do nothing).

> **EXAMPLE:** The picture of using the power of a car gives some idea how this exercise of faith works. We have all of the car's power at our disposal, but we move forward in power only when we press down on the gas pedal, and we stop the car in power only when we press the break pedal. Attempting to obey God's commands is like stepping down on the gas pedal to do what he tells us to do, or stepping down on the break pedal to stop doing what he tells us not to do. The power is released and we have divine assistance in fulfilling our attempt at obedience.

The Blessings of Obedience

Obeying God's commands allows us to experience his blessings. Two commands in particular open the door to those blessings: "repent" and "believe" (Mark 1:15). "Repent" means "to change one's mind." "Believe" means "to consider something to be true and therefore worthy of one's trust."

When we repent and believe the gospel, God gives us the righteousness of God (Romans 4:16, 21, 22-25; 6:16, 19; 10:9-10; 1 Corinthians 15:3-4). This is called positional righteousness or justification. We use what we have been given by obeying his commands through the power of the Holy Spirit. This is called experiential righteousness or sanctification (Romans 6:19). In other words, when we obey we experience the righteousness we have already been given.

By God's grace, we repent and believe the gospel in order to experience the blessing of positional righteousness, the removal of the penalty of sin by complete forgiveness of sins (Romans 4:6-8), the blessing of eternal life (Romans 5:21), and the receiving of the promised Holy Spirit by whom we inherit all of God's blessings and the power to live the abundant life (Ephesians 1:3, 13-14; 1 Corinthians 2:11-14; John 10:10b).

Obedience to every other command of Christ causes us to live righteously (Romans 6:16). When we obey the commands of Christ, we experience the abundant life Jesus came to bring us (John 10:10b). The following verses list some of the blessings that accompany obedient, or righteous, living:

1. **Positional and experiential righteousness (obedient living by the power of the Holy Spirit) protect us from the powers of darkness.** Ephesians 6:14

2. **Experiential righteousness yields peaceful fruit.** Hebrews 12:11

3. **Experiential righteousness yields blessing even when it results in persecution.** 1 Peter 3:14

4. **Experiential righteousness is evidence of being born again.** 1 John 2:29; 3:7

5. **Experiential righteousness blesses the individual.** Proverbs 10:6

6. **Experiential righteousness blesses the family.** Proverbs 3:33b

7. **Experiential righteousness blesses the city.** Proverbs 11:10-11

8. **Experiential righteousness exalts a nation.** Proverbs 14:34

9. **Experiential righteousness reaps a sure reward.** Proverbs 11:18

The word "righteous" or "righteousness" is used 78 times in the New International Version's (NIV) translation of Proverbs. Count the blessings (personal, family, city, nation)!

Jeremiah 4:1-2 (NIV) - Shows that righteousness blesses the nations.

John 17:23 - Righteousness yields a unified testimony to the world concerning God sending His son and loving His people.

The Results of Persistently Obeying the Lord Jesus Christ

1 Corinthians 7:19 (ESV) For neither circumcision counts for anything nor uncircumcision, but keeping the commandments of God.

1 Corinthians 7:19 (GNT) ἡ περιτομὴ οὐδέν ἐστιν καὶ ἡ ἀκροβυστία οὐδέν ἐστιν, ἀλλὰ τήρησις ἐντολῶν θεοῦ.

Define: τήρησις,εως,ἡ [τηρέω] "obeying" - act of observing instruction, keeping, obeying

1. **We make disciples who make disciples when we obey God's commands.** Matthew 28:19-20 - **observe (τήρησις,εως,ἡ [τηρέω] "obey"**

2. **We gain God's provision when we obey His commands.** Matthew 6:33

3. **We gain a growing intimacy with the Lord when we obey Him.** John 14:21, 23

4. **We bear much fruit when we obey God's commands.** John 15:5 (1 John 3:24)

5. **We gain answered prayer when we obey God's commands and pray according to His Word.** John 15:7 (1 John 3:24)

6. **We defeat the enemy when we obey God's commands.** James 4:7

7. **We express love to people and God when we obey His commands.** 1 John 5:2-3

Look it Up

Locate the 150+ commands in the New Testament in addition to the Ten Commandments that are summarized in Matthew 22:37-39.

Resource for Further Study

Need help? Download a copy of **The Commands of Christ ebook** on our website. This ebook contains a list of the Lord's commands in parallel translations to help you study them more effectively.

For more disciple-making resources: *plethosglobal.com*

What Did the Lord Command Us to Do?

The following commands are a few of the more than 150 commands the Lord has given us in the New Testament:

Matthew 28:20 "Teaching them to obey everything I have commanded you."

Matthew 17:5 "Listen to Him [Jesus Christ]."

Matthew 22:37 (see also 1 John 5:3) "Love the Lord your God with all your heart and with all your soul and with all your mind."

Matthew 22:39 (see also 1 John 5:2) "Love your neighbor as yourself."

1 John 5:2-3 - We express love to people and to God by obeying His commands.

MILK & MEAT of the Word ✕

#BuildtheHome

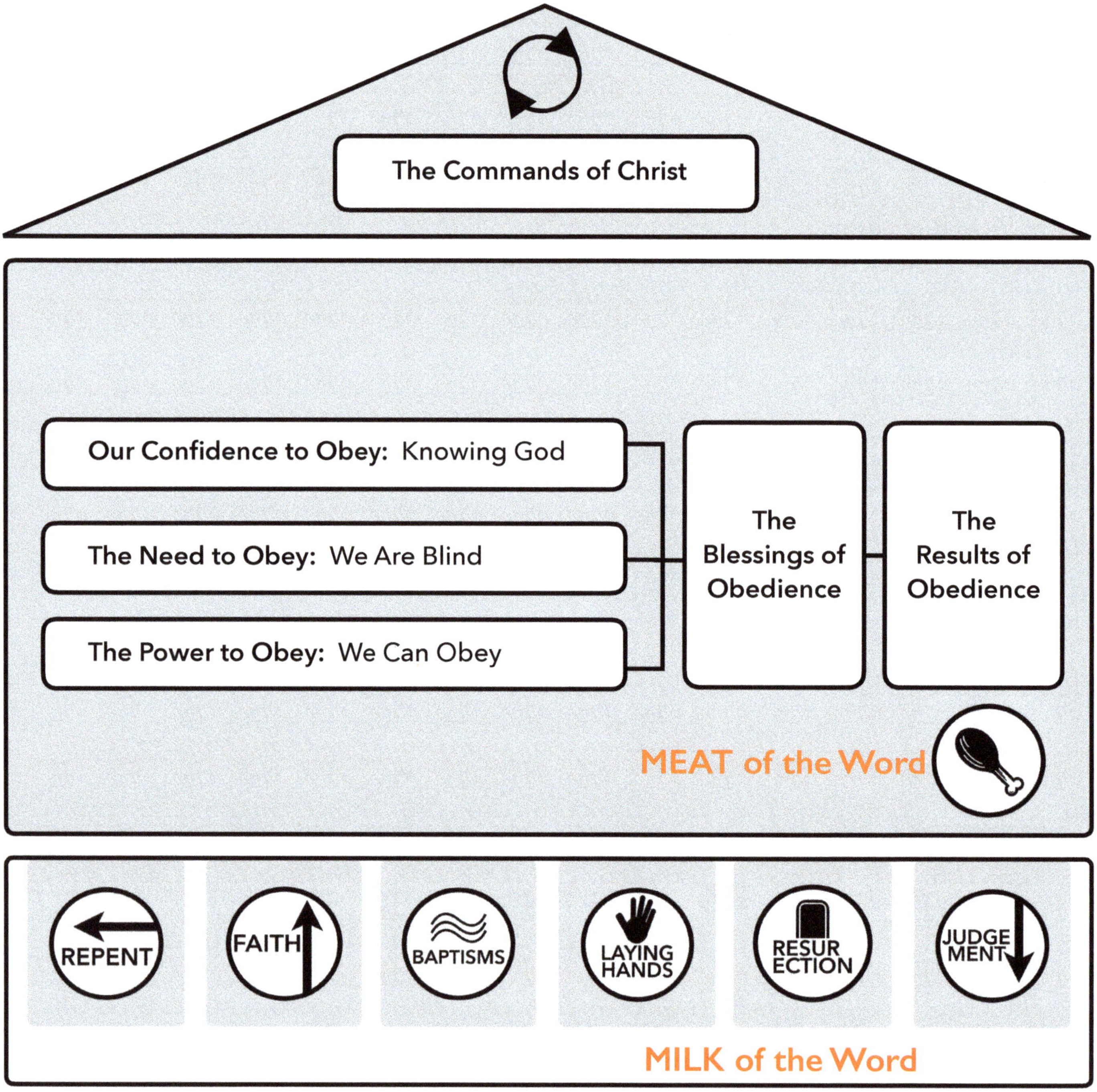

The Commands of Christ

- Our Confidence to Obey: Knowing God
- The Need to Obey: We Are Blind
- The Power to Obey: We Can Obey

- The Blessings of Obedience
- The Results of Obedience

MEAT of the Word

REPENT · FAITH · BAPTISMS · LAYING HANDS · RESURECTION · JUDGEMENT

MILK of the Word

www.ingramcontent.com/pod-product-compliance
Lightning Source LLC
Chambersburg PA
CBHW040750020526
44118CB00042B/2854